THE MEDITERRANEAN

Refresh Diet

COOKBOOK FOR BEGINNERS

100+ Fast, Delicious And Easy To Cook
Mediterranean Recipes For Eating
Healthy Everyday

Nourish and Classy Chef

TABLE OF CONTENTS

INTRODUCTION

Reversing through the endless array of diet options out there can get overwhelming. With so many different diets, it's not hard to get torn between what is healthy and what simply tastes better. But if you're looking for a diet that will provide you with a more robust sense of wellbeing, an improved skin complexion and hair quality, less depression and anxiety (among other side effects), there is one particular diet that many people recommend: the Mediterranean diet.

Mediterranean Diet?

Yes, this diet has been around for thousands of years and is considered to be one of the healthiest diets out there. It's rich in fiber, protein, and various vitamins and minerals, making it an ideal diet for people with underactive thyroid conditions, diabetes, cancer, heart disease, or high blood pressure. If you're looking for a diet that will help you lose weight and keep it off, this is the one you should go for.

I'm normally not a dieter that strictly follows the food pyramid when it comes to healthy eating, and I'm not immune to the occasional fast-food indulgence... but the more I've learned about the Mediterranean diet, the more I learn that it could definitely be a great way to eat healthy without feeling like you're sacrificing anything. I've been able to stay on track with my diet, even through family get-togethers and office holiday parties. In fact, I've been able to enjoy myself at these events without the guilt, since I knew I was doing something good for my body.

The Mediterranean diet isn't about eating specific foods; rather, it's about making smart choices concerning your daily diet. It's all about maintaining an active lifestyle and choosing to live a more fulfilling life.

The Mediterranean diet recommends that you eat a wide variety of foods and incorporate them into each meal.

In fact, according to Dr. Andrew Weil, an expert in the field of alternative medicine, the Mediterranean diet is one of the healthiest diets you can choose to follow. It's also noted by nutritionists as being one of the most effective diet plans out there when it comes to weight loss. With just a few simple changes, you can make the switch to a diet that has helped many people lose weight and maintain a healthier body successfully.

For many years, we have been telling you that eating healthy meals can help you live a longer and healthier life. On the same note, the Mediterranean diet emphasizes living a long life and eating a wide variety of foods that will provide you with a healthy and positive lifestyle. The Mediterranean diet is the best diet to follow if you want to be healthy.

If you want to be healthy but don't want the hassle of counting calories or the carbs you consume, then this is the diet for you.

If you are tired of trying different diets that require a lot of preparation and food restrictions, then consuming foods from a Mediterranean diet cookbook could be a great choice for you.

If you want a diet that can help improve your health, then following the Mediterranean diet is exactly what you need to do.

The Mediterranean diet is quite simple and can be followed by anyone. It has no restrictive rules like the Paleo or Atkins diets. This diet simply encourages you to eat a wide variety of foods while cutting down your intake of sugar, saturated fats, and processed foods.

When you start eating Mediterranean cuisine, you will notice that these dishes are deliciously prepared with only high-quality ingredients. You will also notice that these dishes are simple with easy-to-follow instructions.

While reading this book, you would be able to visit the most beautiful places in the world without leaving your kitchen. With the Mediterranean diet as your guide and this cookbook as your weapon, you will be able to bring the Mediterranean diet right into your kitchen. You will get to know what makes this diet so special and why it is popular even today.

The Mediterranean Diet Cookbook presents a collection of delicious recipes that you can prepare for breakfast, lunch, dinner, and even snacks. You will also be able to enjoy a wide variety of snacks and desserts based on recipes from this cookbook.

Most of the recipes in this book are made from easy-to-find ingredients and do not require any special skill to prepare. The instructions that you will find in this book are easy to follow, and anyone who is experienced in cooking can easily use them to cook great-tasting dishes.

The Mediterranean Diet Cookbook is your guide to a healthy lifestyle. In this book, you will be able to learn how the diet can help you improve your health and live longer. You will also learn about the benefits of consuming this diet. You will learn how to select ingredients that can help you improve your health and prepare a wide variety of healthy and delicious foods.

This book includes more than 100 recipes that all taste great and are as easy to prepare as they can be.

What are you waiting for? Read this book and start a new lifestyle today!

CHAPTER ONE

MEDITERRANEAN DIET

The Mediterranean diet mainly incorporates the healthiest food consumption habits practiced by the people who live in nations that border the Mediterranean Sea. Notably, the Mediterranean diet essentially includes the consumption of vegetables of any kind, nuts, beans, grains, fish, fruits, and unsaturated natural fats, typically olive oil or sunflower oil. These foods provide individuals with huge health benefits; as a result, they have the lowest chances of suffering from chronic illnesses, typically diabetes, cancer, and mental illnesses that can be triggered from consuming unhealthy foods such as red fatty meat.

The Mediterranean diet came out to the limelight in the 1950s when nutrition scientists began to identify the majority of the world's healthiest population emerging from the Mediterranean Sea basin, as opposed to the wealthier nations of the world, mainly the United States of America and the United Kingdom. It prompted researchers to pick interest in establishing the significant reasons for the wellbeing of the Mediterranean population. Therefore, it was eventually identified that the population in the Mediterranean Sea basin and surrounding areas consume more natural foods with little to no caloric content, that normally being the foods mentioned earlier.

In addition, the Mediterranean diet is not just any healthy diet; rather, it is backed by a strong cultural tradition that promotes the consumption of natural foods with fewer calories. Nevertheless, this tradition is further backed by their indulgence and engagement in active physical activity to regulate the amount of fat accumulation in the body. Moreover, the Primary Prevention of Cardiovascular Disease with Mediterranean Diet (PREDIMED) has evidenced the overwhelming positive health effects achieved through adopting the Mediterranean vegetarian diet. However, it is worth noting that the Mediterranean diet approach comes from a traditional angle. The Mediterranean diet has been thoroughly researched in regards to investigating health benefits associated with its consumption.

The Mediterranean diet is the healthiest diet one can rely on. The different cultures within the basin contributed to the emergence of various natural plants as their main source of food, typically olive trees, wheat, grapevine, orange, lemon trees, tomatoes, eggplants, corn, rice, potatoes, asparagus, mangoes, and others. Moreover, the adverse effects of artificially manufactured foods, red meat, and fatty foods have been highly discouraged in the Mediterranean diet. Besides fruits and natural whole foods, the Mediterranean diet is rich with various herbs such as kale, Parmesan, parsley, basil, rosemary, cinnamon, sage, pepper, mint, and nutmeg, which are significant in treating and overcoming the development of severe illness in people. As such, the prevalence of chronic illness in the Mediterranean basin is not as high as it is in other parts of the world, for example, the United States.

However, it is important to note that the Mediterranean diet stands out distinctively among other diets that contain a higher percentage of calories, fat, sugar, and artificially added ingredients. Above and beyond, vegetables such as garlic, chili, onions, tomatoes, among others make the Mediterranean diet flavorful. It is such taste and natural deliciousness and sweetness that has spanned the consumption of Mediterranean diet food. The Mediterranean diet takes various forms of preparation: it can be prepared as a salad with a variety of vegetables, leaves, fruits, and herbs; the fruits can be used for making naturally sweet juice and smoothies; and the grains, corn, potatoes, and rice can be used to prepare healthy whole foods to boost one's energy levels. Seeds also feature commonly in the Mediterranean diet, such as sunflower seeds, pumpkin seeds, sesame seeds, among others.

Nuts are yet another incredible ingredient that elevates the Mediterranean diet to a greater horizon. The varieties of nuts that feature in the Mediterranean diet include but are not limited to: almonds, walnuts, hazelnuts, macadamia, cashew nuts, groundnuts, shell nuts, among others. It is imperative to note that these nuts also provide a healthy source of oil for cooking foods within this diet, mainly groundnut oil, sesame oil, cashew nut oil, and sunflower oil. Besides the nuts, the Mediterranean diet uses legumes for a better taste and health benefits, which includes beans, peas, pulses, chickpeas, peas, peanuts, and groundnuts. The advantage of using legumes is that they are readily available in other parts of the world too, such as Africa, the Americas, Asia, and middle eastern countries. As a result, it's easy to adopt and adhere to a Mediterranean dietary pattern without having to live in the Mediterranean basin.

Although meat is not generally accepted in the Mediterranean diet, the diet still encourages consuming seafood, mainly white flesh fish, oysters, crabs, salmon, sardines, tuna, mackerel, mussels, clams, trout, and shrimp. Fish in the Mediterranean diet is the major source of protein other than poultry. More so, seafood does not have unwanted fats like animal meat does, which can aid the development of cardiovascular disease. Besides, fish oil is encouraged as a substitute to artificially manufactured oil because of its minimal number of calories, thus preventing one from becoming obese. Obesity is usually caused by an accumulation of unused calories in the body, impeding functions.

Nevertheless, there have been considerable comparisons between Mediterranean diet and other healthy diets, especially dietary approaches to stop hypertension. These other dietary approaches focus on how best to control and stop high blood pressure through consuming natural foods. More so, this involves the consumption of fruits, vegetables, fish, and whole grains; especially oats, rye, rice, and wheat. Notably, there is a very slight difference between the two diet plans, and the Mediterranean diet is most preferred because in addition to consuming the foods above, it disallows the consumption of any red or lean meat intake; although sometimes, people compromise and consume small amounts in a month per serving, whereof use of unhealthy foods is substituted with natural oils, typically the ones as mentioned: olive oil, sunflower oil, sesame oil, groundnut oil, and oils from other nuts and vegetables.

The Mediterranean diet could be the world's healthiest diet. Compared to a strict meal plan, it stresses consuming whole foods and daily physical exercise. It is a way of living that is close to the cuisine of countries around the Mediterranean Sea. There is no single diet definition, but you can eat foods mainly based on plants. The Mediterranean diet has been shown by a report published in the New England Journal of Medicine to decrease the risk of cardiac disease, stroke, and death due to heart issues by 30%. To improve fitness, regulate blood sugar, and avoid cardiovascular disease, it should be used as a long-term diet pattern. Many plant-based foods are consumed. Meals are prepared around these foods. Moderate levels of lean meat, fish, seafood, dairy, and eggs are also part of the diet. Cooked foods, desserts, red meat, and white flour goods should be avoided.

Not only is the Mediterranean diet an extreme wealth of food and recipes, but it is also an important point of communication between people and territory: the people of the Mediterranean have already seen their lives on their land, and most products of the diet are born from the land. The laborious selection of products in the Mediterranean lands must guarantee everything that our body requires for working if eaten well. Today, eating has become an important part of our lives. The art of eating well has become a model for the public to pursue. The diet has been one of the most important things to be monitored in the medical profession, preventing many diet therapy disorders and getting gradually recognized by doctors and patients. Its composition is the Mediterranean diet's success. The model that everyone should follow is a diet rich in tradition and association with a single active lifestyle.

The Mediterranean diet is not specific; rather, it is an eating style inspired by Southern European countries' diets. The diet puts together traditional types of food and good practices from the cultures of many different regions, including Greece, Spain, Portugal, Italy, and southern France. Studies have found that there is a reduced incidence of multiple illnesses, including obesity, diabetes, cancer, and cardiovascular disease for people who live in the Mediterranean region or adopt the Mediterranean diet. They are much more likely than people in other areas to live a longer life. New vegetables and fruits, oily fish, unsaturated fats, mild dairy consumption, and a low intake of meat and extra sugar are main components of this diet. Studies also associate these variables with good wellbeing. Many tests have already found that weight loss can be affected by the Mediterranean diet, and it can help one avoid heart problems, strokes, type 2 diabetes, and premature death.

As there are many countries across the Mediterranean Sea, and people in various places could have consumed different diets, there is no "best" way to adopt the Mediterranean diet. With a Mediterranean diet, water can be the go-to beverage. There are also moderate levels of red wine in this diet—about one glass a day. However, this is entirely voluntary, and someone with a history or current alcoholism or issues regulating their intake should avoid wine. Even coffee and tea are appropriate, but sugar-sweetened drinks and fruit juices rich in sugar should be avoided. It is contentious when deciding precisely which foods belong to the Mediterranean diet, partially because there is some variance between many nations. Most researchers have studied this diet rich in balanced plant foods and comparatively low in animal foods. Consuming fish and seafood, however, is recommended at least twice a week. Regular physical exercise, sharing food with other people, and enjoying life are all included in the Mediterranean lifestyle. You should build your diet around organic and unprocessed Mediterranean food.

CHAPTER TWO

WHY IS THE MEDITERRANEAN
DIET SO HEALTHY?

The Mediterranean diet is healthy because you are eating a large number of fruits and vegetables and olive oil, and these types of nutrition are particularly healthy for our bodies. The omega-3 fatty acids found in fish, such as salmon and mackerel, also make this type of cuisine healthy. The foods made from starch and fiber also contain important vitamins and minerals.

Mediterranean cuisine has a preventive effect against heart diseases and obesity, and ultimately, digestion is also promoted. The risk of cancer is also reduced.

If you follow a Mediterranean diet, you can cut your risk of heart attack in half. In addition, your blood pressure is improved, which can lead to a reduction in the risk of stroke. This diet also brings health benefits related to heart disease, coupled with impotence.

Mediterranean cuisine is therefore particularly essential for men, where heart disease and erectile dysfunction could occur.

Mediterranean cuisine protects from all of the above diseases better than a low-fat diet. This type of diet can have an even better effect if you combine it with sports activities. The metabolism and fat burning are significantly increased and stimulated.

The main ingredient of this kitchen is fresh vegetables. As is known, vegetables contain many important vitamins and secondary plants or vital substances.

In summary, the Mediterranean diet has a positive effect on the following problems and diseases:

- Heart disease
- Overweight
- Indigestion
- Cancer
- Blood pressure
- Stroke
- Impotence
- Diabetes
- Dementia

This diet has proven to be much more effective than some medication. Mediterranean cuisine can reduce the risk of developing a large number of different diseases.

Mediterranean Diet/ Health Benefits

The overall demand and recommendation of the consumption and reliance on a Mediterranean diet for a better life is on a significant increase. The reliance on this diet is typical because of the disease prevention properties embedded within Mediterranean natural foods, especially onions, ginger, garlic, rosemary, kale, lemon, apple, papaya, oranges, olives, avocado, among many other plants. Moreover, it contributes remarkably to the prevention and management of minor and chronic illness, mainly cardiovascular disease, diabetes, hypertension, cancer, and sickle cell. Furthermore, the Mediterranean diet has a weighty and striking impact on the survival of these delicate patients. The reduction of atherosclerosis and risk of fatal complications are minimized if the person experiencing these illnesses sticks to their Mediterranean dietary pattern consistently. Unlike artificially manufactured drugs, Mediterranean diets have no adverse side effects on the body; instead, they help in building and boosting the body's immunity that guards you from an external attack.

The Mediterranean diet requires no calorie intake calculation because the percentage of calories in these natural plants is just the amount that the body needs; therefore, consumption is quite harmless. This can be achieved by simply substituting fatty oils with olive, groundnut, sunflower, or shell nut oils. Additionally, refraining from taking manufactured sugars will also help control the calorie levels in your body. It is rather difficult to consume food that is not fresh, especially packed foods. Mediterranean foods are harvested from the garden and go straight to the saucepan for a delicious meal with all the food values intact. Also, the Mediterranean diet has the spiciest natural flavors, including ginger, garlic, coriander, cilantro, bay leaves, lemongrass, pepper, and lemon. All you have to do is select what suits your taste and preference; add as much as you can, as it is all good for your health and will cause no adverse health complications.

Undoubtedly, preparing Mediterranean food is quite simple to make within the shortest time possible. First, getting the ingredients for your Mediterranean diet is simple in visiting a store for fresh vegetables, fruits, and whole foods. Similarly, growing these plants in your backyard using a hydroponic system of cultivation is easy, and you will not need chunks of land to do that. Most of these plants can be consumed raw. The fruits, some vegetables, and greens can be eaten raw as you prepare the main course. Besides the easy preparation and lack of calorie intake, the Mediterranean diet is a striking methodology for achieving quick and rapid weight loss. Nonetheless, you should still not overconsume any food in large quantities, as overconsumption of anything is bad. There is a likelihood of suffering from constipation or over-congestion of food in the stocking, which can cause significant discomfort for yourself.

Heart Health

Generally, the ever-increasing rate of medical heart conditions can be attributed to the kind of food we consume every day. As a result, the population that lives in the poorer areas of the world, typically in the

Mediterranean Sea basin, have had a lower rate of heart conditions reported, as opposed to their counterparts in urban centers with access to various unhealthy foods. The Mediterranean diet enables an individual to maintain the required level of cholesterol in the body, thus reducing the risk of high blood pressure and obesity. Furthermore, fat is a primary source of calories, hence one's restriction to only consuming Mediterranean diet can limit the accumulation of calories in the body.

Protection from Diseases

The Mediterranean diet is focused on plant food with a rich source of antioxidants. Antioxidants help protect the body from illness attacks. Furthermore, these antioxidants can help build a strong defense together with the body's immune system, thereby preventing attacks from several potential illnesses. Moreover, antioxidants are also significant in influencing a person's mental and physical health. The chances of stroke and diabetes are also remarkably lower with the Mediterranean diet, since it, by nature, lowers and regulates blood glucose levels.

Diabetes

The Mediterranean diet may not entirely prevent diabetes; it has a high chance of preventing type 2 diabetes, common in adults, and it can help in effectively managing glucose levels of those who already have diabetes. However, the ability of the Mediterranean diet to combat type 2 diabetes also has signified that it can minimize chances of cardiovascular diseases which, in most cases occur together with diabetes. Above and beyond, the foods that make the Mediterranean diet are recommended for diabetic patients, indicating that it is healthier and can help partially regulate the blood glucose level of diabetic patients.

Mediterranean Diet Recipes

There are several Mediterranean diet recipes, ranging from fruit and juice recipes to whole grain or meal recipes. These recipes, whether easy to make, all have incredible health benefits and will be irresistibly delicious and tasty for any meal. Furthermore, these recipes are fresh and whole with their natural flavors and nutrients. In a nutshell, the Mediterranean recipes include but are not limited to the following.

Fruit Mediterranean Diet Recipes

Undoubtedly, fruits are the omega and an outstanding source of vitamins, which are important in building the immune system. They are also an important source of antioxidants.

You already know that the Mediterranean cuisine consists primarily of dishes based on fresh fruit and vegetables. But what are the advantages of the individual components?

Fresh Vegetables

The main ingredient of this diet is fresh vegetables. As is known, vegetables contain many important vitamins and secondary plants or vital substances.

When preparing the vegetables, you should make sure you do not cook them in water, but steam them with a little liquid. As a result, the valuable ingredients such as vitamins will not be lost through the heat.

Make sure that you always buy and prepare your vegetables fresh. Do not use frozen vegetables, as they have already lost nutrients and vitamins due to freezing.

Of course, you can also cook your vegetables completely fat-free in the wok. If you want to lose weight, it would be a good alternative to the preparation with olive oil in the pan. Olive oil is not an unhealthy fat, but as with all food, it is best consumed in moderation.

Fish

Fish such as salmon, mackerel, and herring are rich in omega-3 fatty acids. These lower blood pressure and protect the walls of the blood vessels.

Lean fish would be, for example, pike perch or cod. This in turn saves calories, which benefits the weight loss process. Under no circumstances should you bread or fry the fish when cooking for this diet.

Roasting at moderate to medium temperatures is important because high temperatures can change the taste of cold-pressed oils or destroy important ingredients.

Bread, Pasta, Rice, etc.

The Mediterranean kitchen offers hardly any food without bread to eat with it. However, the bread is eaten without toppings. Pasta, rice, potatoes, millet, bulgur, corn grits in the form of polenta, and couscous are all also part of Mediterranean cuisine.

However, these foods are only consumed in smaller quantities as side dishes. The main component of the meal is still fresh vegetables.

CHAPTER THREE

BASIC PRINCIPLES OF THE DIET

Understanding Nutrition Labels

L ook for the short ingredient list: The first ingredient is usually the bulk of the food, which is listed by weight. Put an ingredient back on the shelf if you don't recognize it. Using products containing no more than five ingredients where necessary. Unnecessary extras, such as artificial preservatives, are more likely to blame for the longer ingredient list.

Check serving sizes: Frequently, packages contain more than one serving. Think about how many calories and sugar are stored in a single container. Thus, you must first decide the serving amount.

Watch calorie counts: It's important to verify the calorie count on the package because it'll help you adhere to the Mediterranean diet schedule.

Avoid fats: It's important to exclude foods that contain entirely hydrogenated or partly hydrogenated oils from your diet.

Check the Percentage of daily value: The daily value of a packaged item will tell you the number of nutrients in each serving.

Get more of these nutrients: Look for calcium, iron, fiber, vitamin A, and vitamin C.

The Label Explained

- Serving information at the top provides the size of one serving and per container.
- Check the total calories per serving and container.
- Limit certain nutrients from your diet.
- Provide yourself with plenty of beneficial nutrients.
- Understand the percentage of the daily value section.

Avoid These Foods

- **Added sugar:** Ice cream, candy, regular soda, among many others.
- **Refined oils:** Canola oil, cottonseed oil, soybean oil, etc.
- **Trans fats**: Found in various processed foods such as margarine, added sugar, ice cream, candy, table sugar, soda, added sugars, sugar-sweetened beverages, refined grains, and other highly processed foods.
- **Processed meat products:** Hot dogs, processed sausages, and bacon.
- **Refined grains:** Pasta made with refined wheat, white bread.

Note if you are pregnant: You should avoid some of the oily fish such as swordfish, shark, and tuna because some may contain low levels of toxic heavy metals.

Foods You Can Eat

- **Seafood and fish:** Mussels, clams, crab, prawns, oysters, shrimp, tuna, mackerel, salmon, trout, sardines, anchovies, and more.

- **Poultry**: Turkey, duck, chicken, and more.

- **Eggs**: Duck, quail, and chicken eggs.

- **Dairy products:** Contain calcium, B12, and vitamin A: Greek yogurt, regular yogurt, cheese, among others.

- **Tubers**: Yams, turnips, potatoes, sweet potatoes, etc.

- **Vegetables**: Another excellent choice for fiber and antioxidants: Cucumbers, carrots, Brussels sprouts, tomatoes, onions, broccoli, cauliflower, spinach, kale, eggplant, artichokes, fennel, etc.

- **Seeds and nuts**: Provide minerals, vitamins, fiber, and protein: Macadamia nuts, cashews, pumpkin seeds, sunflower seeds, hazelnuts, chestnuts, Brazil nuts, walnuts, almonds, pumpkin seeds, sesame, poppy, and more.

- **Fruits:** Excellent vitamin C choices, antioxidants, and fiber: Peaches, bananas, apples, figs, dates, pears, oranges, strawberries, melons, grapes, etc.

- Spices and Herbs: Cinnamon, garlic, pepper, nutmeg, rosemary, sage, mint, basil, parsley, etc.

- **Whole Grains**: Whole grain bread and pasta, buckwheat, whole wheat, barley, corn, whole oats, rye, quinoa, bulgur, couscous.

- **Legumes:** Provide vitamins, fiber, carbohydrates, and protein: Chickpeas, pulses, beans, lentils, peanuts, peas.

- **Healthy Fats**: Avocado oil, avocados, and olives are excellent fats. Olive oil contains monounsaturated fat, which can assist in the removal of "bad" cholesterol. For some of the world's healthiest populations, the oil has been the conventional fat. Much research has shown that the antioxidants and fatty acids in the product may increase the chance of heart disease.

- When buying olive oil, bear in mind that it may have been harvested from the olives using chemicals or diluted with cheaper oils like canola or soybean. You should differentiate between refined or light olive oils and regular olive oils. Extra virgin olive oil is recommended as part of the Mediterranean diet because it has been standardized for purity using natural methods and has superior sensory qualities like taste and scent. The oil contains several phenolic antioxidants, so it's healthy for you.

- **Beverage options**: Maintaining a healthy body requires lots of water, and the Mediterranean diet plan is no exception. Tea and coffee are appropriate, but fruit juices and sugar-sweetened drinks with high sugar content should be avoided.

- **White meats:** White meats contain many minerals, protein, and vitamins, but you should remove any visible fat and the skin.

- **Potatoes**: Potatoes are classified in the tubers class because they are a healthy choice, but how they are cooked will have a significant effect. Potassium, vitamin B, vitamin C, and some fiber nutrients are all provided. You should bear in mind that they contain a lot of starch that can easily be transformed to glucose, which can be dangerous and put you at risk for type 2 diabetes. Cook them with less effort, meaning baking, boiling, or mashing them without butter.

- **Desserts and Sweets:** Biscuits, cookies, and sweets should only be eaten in small quantities as a special treat. Sugar not only raises your potential for type 2 diabetes, but it can also lead to tooth decay. They also produce higher levels of saturated fat. You will get some nutritious value, but as a rule, keep your servings small.

To Consume in Moderation

- Eggs
- Poultry
- Milk
- Butter
- Yogurt
- Cheese

Improve the Flavor of Foods

When on the diet, you can add flavor and aroma to your food by using herbs and spices. It will also help you cut back on the amount of salt and fat you use while cooking your meals. Chiles, lavender, tarragon, savory, sumac, and zaatar are some spices and herbs that conform to the Mediterranean diet's requirements.

These are a few more ways you can benefit from spices and herbs:

Anise: Can aid digestion while reducing nausea and relieving cramps. After a meal, make some anise tea to help relieve indigestion, bloating, and constipation.

Bay leaf: Bay leaves contain magnesium, calcium, potassium, and vitamins A and C. You are promoting your general health, and it is also proven to be useful in treating migraines.

Basil: Helps with digestion, gastric disorders, and flatulence control. You can also greatly manage your diabetes, preserve your heart wellbeing, and reduce depression and anxiety when using basil. Try rubbing them onto your scalp after shampooing the next time you have dandruff. The additives assist in removing dandruff and dry skin.

Black pepper: Pepper aids nutrient absorption in the tissues in the body, stimulates metabolism, and increases digestion. Pepper's key ingredient is a pipeline, which gives it its pungent taste. It can increase fat metabolism by up to 8% for many hours after intake. It's used in all of your balanced Mediterranean dishes, as you'll see.

Cayenne pepper: Capsaicin, a naturally occurring compound that gives peppers their fiery heat, is the secret ingredient in cayenne. This improves your metabolism for a brief period. Peppers are also high in vitamins, serve as an appetite controller, help with digestion, and are healthy for your heart.

Sweet and spicy cloves: For a spicy taste, add cloves to hot tea. Cloves include antiseptic and germicidal ingredients that can aid with a range of pains, including arthritis, gum and tooth pain, stomach conditions, and infection prevention. Clove oil should be used as an antiseptic for fungal infections, itchy rashes, cuts, and burns. Cloves' fragrance alone can help stimulate mental imagination.

Ground chia seeds: The seeds can absorb liquid up to 11 times their own weight. Before using them in your recipes, make sure to soak them in plenty of water for at least five minutes; otherwise, you will feel some digestive problems after eating them. Make sure you remain hydrated.

Cumin: Cumin has been described as spicy, earthy, nutty, and warm in flavor. It's been used as traditional medicine for a long time. It can aid digestion and reduce the risk of foodborne illnesses. It will also help you lose weight and regulate your cholesterol and blood sugar levels.

Fennel: Potassium, phosphorus, vitamin A, calcium, vitamin C, copper, vitamin B6, and magnesium are all nutrients present in fennel. Phosphate and calcium are ideal for bone structure; iron and zinc are important for collagen production and boosting bone health. Vitamin C, folate, potassium, and fiber, both of which are contained in fennel, protect your heart health.

Garlic: Garlic is the best when it comes to reducing blood sugar and inducing weight loss. It assists in appetite management.

Ginger: Ginger is a diuretic that helps you remove more urine. It's also known for its cholesterol-fighting properties, as well as its ability to improve metabolism and mobility. Ginger can help fight bloating.

Marjoram: This is used in the diet to promote healthy digestion, assist with type 2 diabetes management, correct hormone imbalances, and promote restful sleep and a calm mind.

Mint: Mint helps in treating nasal congestion, nausea, dizziness, and headaches. It helps improve blood circulation, improves dental health, and helps with colic in infants. Mint helps prevent dandruff and pesky head lice.

Oregano: Oregano is easy to introduce into your diet; it is rich in antioxidants and can assist in fighting against bacteria. Oregano is also useful in treating the common cold because it assists in reducing infections, killing intestinal bacteria, and relieving menstrual cramps. One major advantage is that it delivers nutrients to the body to aid weight control and digestion.

Parsley: Using its high amounts of apigenin, a flavonoid, will help the skin, prostate, and digestive system. It has strong antioxidant and inflammatory powers, as well as anti-cancer properties.

Rosemary: This spice helps increase hair growth, relieve pain, ease stress, and reduce joint inflammation.

Sage: The sage plant's leaves are also used in medicine. It's a perfect way to get rid of diarrhea, abdominal pain or gastritis, heartburn, and gas or flatulence. It may also benefit patients with depression, Alzheimer's disease, memory loss, among several other illnesses.

Tarragon: The tarragon spice is an excellent choice for maintaining your blood sugar levels, keeping your heart healthy, reducing inflammation symptoms, improving digestive functions, improving central nervous system conditions, and supporting healthier eyes.

Thyme: Thyme is another spice that has been used for protection against the Black Death and embalming throughout history. It's not a pretty dinner suggestion, but it's fascinating nonetheless. It's also believed to have antibacterial and insecticidal properties. It may be used as an essential oil, dried herb, or fresh herb.

You'll find that the ingredients in your new meal plan have a long list of spices in them. They not only enhance the flavor of your food, but they also improve your wellbeing!

FAQs

Does the Mediterranean diet let me eat carbs?
The Mediterranean diet does not cut out any food groups or macronutrients. However, you need to be wise about the kind of carbohydrates you put in your mouth. I think you can agree that eating chips as a form of carbohydrates is not a good idea. Of course, you can eat brown rice, brown pasta, etc.

Can I still eat dessert?

The good news is yes, you can. However, you need to make sure you eat desserts in moderation. The key is to keep an eye on your sugar intake. Also, you can always opt for sweet fruits with Greek yogurt for dessert.

Is the Mediterranean diet expensive?

If you consider that you will mainly be eating fresh produce, beans, and whole grains, I say no. This diet is not expensive. If you compare it to other diets that cut out some food groups or focus on protein, you are likely to save a lot of money on this diet. Another thing is that you will not be eating out as much as you used to.

Will I lose weight on the Mediterranean diet?

Yes; if you are carrying some excess weight, you will shed some weight. There is no need to count calories on this diet. However, if you have been eating a high-calorie diet, the Mediterranean diet will have you on a calorie deficit, which will make you lose weight. Another thing to consider is that this diet is nutrient filled, so you will feel full longer.

Can I still drink coffee?

Drinking coffee is allowed with this diet. Again, you need to keep an eye on your sugar intake. If you are used to getting your coffee at a coffee shop for instance, opt for something sugar-free.

CHAPTER FOUR

HEALTHY HABITS FOR
DIET SUCCESS

In order to learn how to follow the Mediterranean diet and enjoy better health, you need to make several changes in your lifestyle. You need to make a few modifications in the way you eat and live. In this book, you will learn how to incorporate some of these changes into your daily activities.

Once you have made these changes in your lifestyle, you will be able to enjoy the benefits and advantages of the Mediterranean diet for good without having to go through too much trial and error.

Achieving healthy habits is not an easy task, and most people do not stick to these habits for long. However, if you are determined enough, then you can learn to develop good healthy habits that will help you improve your health. Here are the healthy habits that will help you enjoy the Mediterranean way of eating.

Eat Breakfast Every Day

Eating breakfast is an essential part of the Mediterranean diet because it helps you feel full and energized throughout the day. If you skip breakfast, then you are more likely to snack later in the day, which can affect your weight.

Everyone knows that breakfast is the most important meal of the day, but many people still choose to skip it. Skipping meals, unlike with intermittent fasting, which is a completely different diet concept, is bad for you because you are inclined to be ravenous at your next meal. By being so hungry, you are bound to eat more than your average portion, meaning a higher calorie intake.

Eating slowly and consciously goes a long way in allowing our bodies to gauge when we have had enough. You will be surprised at how little you actually need to feel full.

Try eating more often throughout the day, striving for five meals. Start with breakfast, have a snack, then lunch, then another snack, and finish with dinner.

Eat Fish Every Week

Fish is an excellent source of protein that can help you lose weight and maintain a healthy body. When you eat fish regularly, it lowers your risk of developing several diseases. The Mediterranean diet is rich in omega-3 fatty acids, which are found in fish.

Start Cooking with Olive Oil

If you want to enjoy a Mediterranean diet, then you need to start cooking with olive oil. It is one of the most important ingredients in this diet. When you cook with olive oil, you reduce the amount of saturated fat in your diet. The healthy fats in olive oil can help you lose weight and are essential for the proper functioning of your body.

Stay Away from Quick Fixes

If you want to improve your health, then you need to stop eating fast food. You may believe you are saving time because fast food is ready to eat and does not require much preparation; however, the truth is that it takes more time for your body to digest the bad calories from fast food than it would take to prepare a quick, healthy meal in your kitchen.

Fast food is too rich in fat and can quickly fill your belly. The excess fat will also take hours for your body to burn.

If you want to enjoy the benefits of a Mediterranean diet, then you will need to get rid of your love for fast food.

Eat Plenty of Fruits and Vegetables

Fruits and vegetables are an excellent source of fiber. Fiber can help you feel full for hours and will prevent you from eating too much food. Fruit is also rich in vitamins and minerals, which are essential for a healthy body.

Use Herbs Instead of Salt

Herbs are an essential ingredient to the Mediterranean diet. If you want to prepare the tasty dishes that are part of this diet, then you should have on hand fresh herbs for seasoning your meals. Herbs are high in vitamins and minerals, and they also taste delicious. You can find them in most supermarkets or at specialty food shops.

Herbs are a great way to add flavor to your foods without adding any calories. Most herbs have some type of health benefit, and they can easily be grown at home. You don't need much space, just a small pot of water or terrarium. It is best to choose herbs with pretty flower petals that will also look good on the table.

Keep an Eye on Your Weight

The Mediterranean diet will help you lose weight without putting your health at risk. The diet is rich in healthy fats that are good for your body and can aid in regulating your cholesterol levels. The diet is also rich in fiber that can help you feel full for hours.

If your weight ever starts to increase, then you should consider reducing your portions or adding more physical activity to your daily activities. Exercising every day can help you lose weight, but only until you reach your goal. After that, you can go back to your old routine and continue to lose weight or start a new one.

Eat a Varied Diet

Switch up your diet by eating a variety of fresh fruits and vegetables, lean proteins, and whole grains. When you eat food that is part of the Mediterranean diet, it does not have to be boring. It's important to understand that a diet should become a way of life, thus it shouldn't feel like you are on one.

Binge eating also happens when we say no to particular foods, and on the day we say yes to a chocolate bar, we end up eating far too much because we denied ourselves for so long. Make smart choices, but you don't necessarily have to say no to everything. You won't have much success during or after your diet if you do.

The Mediterranean diet is full of variety, and you can choose from several recipes to prepare for breakfast, lunch, dinner, and snacks. You should try all the different recipes in your favorite cookbooks until you find your favorites.

Your healthy lifestyle will start when you learn how to prepare healthy meals for yourself and your family. Join hundreds of other people who have enjoyed the benefits of following a healthy Mediterranean diet.

Avoiding the grains and bread that are part of this diet will be one of the most difficult changes that you will need to make in your lifestyle, but it is definitely an achievable goal. The problem is that many people love to eat bread and other carb-rich foods. Most people have a very hard time cutting out these foods from their diet.

The good news is that you do not have to cut out all the carbs from your diet. It is a lot easier to avoid bread and other carb-rich foods that are part of the typical American diet than it is to cut out carbs completely.

If you have already enjoyed the benefits of a low-carb diet, then you know that carb cravings can be a terrible thing. Many people have tried to eliminate carbs from their diet, though they have been unable to stick to it. However, when you learn how to eat the Mediterranean way, you can easily cut down your carb consumption and still enjoy delicious food.

If you want to enjoy the Mediterranean diet, then you will have to learn how to incorporate healthy habits into your lifestyle. Once you learn how to develop and maintain these habits, you can continue enjoying the benefits of this diet for a long time.

Make It a Lifestyle Change

Diets come and go, and so do the pounds. The constant battles we have with diets make them harder to stick with, but the truth is, it shouldn't have to be this hard for anybody. The reason most diets fail is that they control us by making us cast aside the way we are used to living—no dinner dates, no drinks with friends, and no ice cream on the beach with the kids. Many times, healthier foods come at a higher price, meaning that people are also less inclined to follow through with it due to the impact it has on the household budget.

The best decision you can make is adopt your new way of eating as part of your lifestyle. The Mediterranean diet is just that: a lifestyle, guaranteeing you the opportunity to live your life saying yes to all things that make your heart and gut happy.

We live in the 21st century, which makes accessing the Internet a breeze. The web has a wealth of information on how to incorporate new changes into your life and stick with them.

Carry on and Stay Motivated

Failure is a part of life and is not the end of the world, especially in the diet department. Learn to become aware of the diet faux pas you might have committed the week prior that would cause the scale to climb. Never quit, always keep yourself motivated, and most importantly, if you do gain one or two pounds, get yourself back on the diet train as quickly as possible to restore your previous weight.

Eating Mindfully

We have all heard how to live mindfully and incorporate meditation into our lives to better handle our stress and anxiety. But what does it mean to eat mindfully? Eating mindfully is the art of paying attention to when you reach for food—is it because you are truly hungry, or is it because you are bored, experiencing depressive thoughts, or stressed?

Eating mindfully goes a long way in addressing bad eating habits that we ourselves have created. How many times do you open the pantry or refrigerator door and stare brainlessly at it? I think many of us do this. Learn to recognize food triggers related to other anxieties and stressors, rather than true hunger pangs. If you find yourself seeking refuge in food for the wrong reasons, go for a walk, talk to a friend, read a magazine, and then return to normalcy. Over time, this conditioning will help you only eat when you need to and not out of anxiety.

Mindful eating also involves paying attention to what you are putting into your body. Next time you find a plate of food in front of yourself, think about the colors and where the food came from, and feel yourself being thankful for having the luxury to enjoy a delicious meal. Secondly, between each bite, be sure to set your knife and fork down. This will allow your body to register the food and properly gauge when it is full.

How to Stay on the Mediterranean Diet

If you are going to be successful on this diet, you will need to plan. Failure to plan is planning to fail. You need to have a clear plan that will guide you going forward. Ask yourself why you are adopting the diet; what is it that you want to achieve? Then you will need to write these goals down somewhere in reach. Determine what you would want to get out of the diet. Is it weight loss? Overall health? Illness prevention? Whatever it is, write it down. If you write down your goals, you will be encouraged to move forward when you achieve even just a little bit. However, be careful to set realistic and achievable goals for yourself. Yes, ideally you would want to attain great leaps of success, but the best way to plan is to take small steps toward your goal. Then, you would need to commit each day of your week toward reaching that goal. Set a reminder on your phone if you have to. Maybe organize the times you prepare your daily meals on a to-do list with alarm reminders to remind you to put some fresh vegetables into your meals and some fruit with your breakfast. No matter what, remember not to quit. Even if you fail one day, bounce back and commit to the diet again the next day or two days later. Have a plan A, and ask yourself what it would take to make the diet a delicious experience for you. If Plan A fails, then go for Plan B. Maybe make Plan A stricter than Plan B.

Take It Slow

Start slow if you have to. There is no rush, and you are likely to enjoy the diet if you ease into it. I know you may want to go into it headfirst. It is perfectly okay to try it that way, but if you know that you have had a lot of failure with previous diets, I recommend that you take this one slowly. Consider replacing a large portion of your plate with vegetables instead of rice, and then alternate days. Have a Mediterranean meal one day and your normal meal on the next. Introduce eating fruit with your cereals. Maybe add some berries or bananas to your oatmeal in the morning. These small steps are here to introduce your tastebuds to a new way of eating. Really, it is to change your mindset around food gradually. If you do not rush yourself, you will find that you will crave the Mediterranean dishes, which is the plan. You can start by enjoying smoothies and shakes. Just make sure you do not make them too sweet. Try to enjoy your meals with their natural taste. It is a refreshing experience once you get used to it. Remember not to weigh your success by just weight loss. Remember that you undertaking this diet is a healthy lifestyle change, and it is a success on its own. Also, even if you cheat for a day or two, you are doing well still because you can go back to the diet. If you compare your diet before the Mediterranean diet, you will understand what I am saying. You are doing far better falling on and off it than you would be if you were eating how you used to.

CHAPTER FIVE

GETTING STARTED WITH THE
MEDITERRANEAN DIET

Your Goals

B efore you get started with this diet, spend some time coming up with goals you wish to achieve. Your goals will determine your level of motivation whenever you decide to follow a diet. Perhaps you want to lose weight, or maybe you want to improve your overall health. Regardless of your goals, it is quintessential that you know what you wish to achieve from the diet. If you don't have any goals, it becomes difficult to stay on track in the long run.

Pick a Date

Once you know your goal, you should work on setting a timeline. Select a date you want to start this diet. Don't be in a rush, and don't think you can get started with this diet right away. It takes a while to prepare your mind and body for the diet you wish to follow. The Mediterranean diet doesn't require any drastic dietary changes; however, if your current diet is rich in processed foods and sugars, your body will have to take time to adjust to this new diet. Therefore, pick a date and ensure you start your diet on that particular date. Don't make any excuses, and don't try to put it off until a later date. If you keep telling yourself that you can start this diet tomorrow, then tomorrow will never come. Take a calendar, mark the date, and get started.

Take the First Step

Once you have made up your mind about this diet, it is time to get started. Don't be afraid; instead, think of it as a stepping stone toward better health. If you get scared, remind yourself of the goals you wish to achieve from this diet. It will make it easier to keep going.

Clean Your Pantry

Before you start this diet, make sure to clean your pantry. Go through the Mediterranean diet shopping list given in the next section and make a list of all the ingredients you will require. Once you have this list, shop for groceries. Make sure to get rid of any other items that don't fit the Mediterranean diet eating protocols—that means processed foods, unhealthy carbs, and sugary treats. Think of it as spring cleaning for your kitchen. It is quintessential that you do this because if you're surrounded by temptations all the time, the chances of giving in to your urges to eat unhealthy food will increase. Out of sight, out of mind is the best approach when it comes to junk food.

Make the Transition

As mentioned in the previous point, if your diet is predominantly rich in processed food and sugar, it might be a little tricky to shift to any other diet. You might not know this, but a diet rich in sugar is quite addictive. Therefore, there are two ways in which you can change your diet. You can either go cold turkey or make a slow transition to the new diet. Slowly start eliminating all unhealthy foods from your diet while incorporating Mediterranean diet-friendly foods. This way, you are conditioning your mind and body to get used to the new diet. Give yourself at least two to three weeks before coming to any conclusions about this diet.

Support System

You must have a support system in place if you want to stick to this diet in the long term. Let go of the "I will just wing it" attitude. There will be days when you will have little to no motivation. This is where your support system comes into the picture. Whenever you believe you don't have the motivation to keep going, you can depend on your support system. Your support system can include your partner, loved ones, friends, or anyone else you want. Talk to them about your reasons for following the diet and tell them what you wish to achieve. By doing this, you are making yourself accountable to someone else. This, in turn, increases your motivation to stick to this diet. You can always go online and get in touch with those who are following the same diet as you.

Be Patient

A common mistake a lot of dieters make is that they are always in a hurry. Making any sort of dietary change is not easy, and it takes time. Not just time, but consistency as well. Don't think that you'll be able to shed all those extra pounds overnight. After all, you didn't gain all that extra weight within a day or two. Thus, you can't expect yourself to get rid of it in a literal snap. Whenever you make a dietary change, you might notice certain fluctuations in your energy levels. This happens because your body is trying to get used to the new diet. So, don't be upset with yourself if you can exercise as vigorously as you used to. Within two to three weeks, your energy levels will stabilize, your body will get used to the new diet, and you will be able to exercise the way you want. Until then, be patient and don't weigh yourself daily. It might be tempting to see whether you've lost any weight daily, but it is not practical. There will be days when the scale doesn't fluctuate like you want it to. Make it a point to weigh yourself every week; it will help keep track of your progress.

Shopping List

Use this basic shopping list whenever you shop for groceries. Ensure that you stock your pantry with all these ingredients and get rid of other items, which will not be suitable for your diet. Your shopping list must include:

1. Veggies like kale, garlic, spinach, arugula, onions, carrots
2. Fruits like grapes, oranges, apples, bananas
3. Berries like blueberries, strawberries, raspberries
4. Frozen veggies
5. Grains like whole-grain pasta, whole-grain breads
6. Legumes like beans, lentils, chickpeas
7. Nuts like walnuts, cashews, almonds
8. Seeds like pumpkin seeds, sunflower seeds
9. Condiments like turmeric, cinnamon, salt, pepper
10. Shrimp, shellfish
11. Fish like mackerel, trout, tuna, salmon, sardines
12. Cheese, yogurt, Greek yogurt
13. Potatoes, sweet potatoes
14. Chicken
15. Eggs
16. Olives
17. Olive oil, avocado oil

If you buy healthy and adequate ingredients, you will most certainly eat the right foods and definitely stay on your diet.

Tricks and Tips that Will Make Things Easier

- Keeping in mind that you cannot eat red meat, you can replace it with salmon. It will satisfy your cravings, but it will allow you to stay on your diet.
- Make sure you always have olive oil at hand. You have to forget about using butter if you are on the Mediterranean diet, but you can replace it with the extra virgin olive oil.
- Give up consuming sodas and replace them with some red wine. Cut out the sweet drinks from your diet and try one glass of red wine instead.
- Replace white rice with brown rice. The Mediterranean diet allows you to continue to eat rice, but make sure you replace the white rice with brown. Consume whole grains like buckwheat, corn, and quinoa.

- Your snacks should mainly contain fruits. Consume more citrus, melons, berries, and grapes. You can also try seeds as a Mediterranean diet snack, but fruit would be a better option.
- Exercise a lot and drink plenty of water. This is a main principle to follow if you are on a Mediterranean diet. It will help you look better and feel amazing. That's a fact!
- Another great idea to keep in mind when you are on such a diet is to make a shopping list like the one above. It will help you buy the right ingredients. Choose organic products if you can, but only if they suit your budget.
- You must keep your body hydrated. Regardless of the dietary changes you make, the one thing you must always concentrate on is proper hydration. When your body is hydrated, all the toxins present within will be flushed out. Not just this, but it also helps improve the health of your skin. You must consume at least eight glasses of water daily. Also, when you're transitioning to this diet or making any dietary changes, hunger pangs are quite common. To keep hunger pangs at bay, ensure that you are drinking lots of water.

COLOR RECIPE IMAGES

We understand, you want recipes in this book with their color images. However, **if we add images of all recipes, the printing cost of this book will be too high** and it won't be affordable to all.

We wanted this book to be priced in a way that everyone can buy it. So, we decided not to add any recipe image in this book.

But this doesn't mean you can't access these images. To make it easier, **we've made IMAGES OF ALL RECIPES available in a PDF format which you can download anytime for free.**

The PDF has color images of all the recipes we listed in this book. **You can download the PDF by visiting to the below URL.**

www.nourishandclassychef.com/m-diet-images

Hope it helps.

CHAPTER SIX

BREAKFAST RECIPES

1. MEDITERRANEAN OMELET

Preparation Time: 7 minutes

Cooking Time: 10-12 minutes

Servings: 2

Ingredients:

- 2 tsp. extra virgin olive oil
- 1 garlic clove
- ½ red bell pepper
- ½ yellow bell pepper
- ¼ cup thinly sliced red onion
- 2 tbsp. chopped fresh basil
- 2 tbsp. chopped fresh parsley
- ½ tsp. salt
- ½ tsp. black pepper
- 4 large eggs, beaten

Directions:

1. In a big, heavy skillet, cook 1 tsp. of the olive oil over medium heat.

2. Add the garlic, peppers, and onion to the pan and sauté, stirring frequently, for 5 minutes.
3. Add the basil, parsley, salt, and pepper, increase the heat to medium-high, and sauté for 2 minutes. Slide the vegetable mixture onto a plate and return the pan to the heat.
4. Heat the remaining 1 tsp. olive oil in the same pan and pour in the beaten eggs, tilting the pan to coat evenly. Cook the eggs just until the edges are bubbly and all but the center is dry, 3 to 5 minutes.
5. Either flip the omelet or use a spatula to turn it over.
6. Spoon the vegetable mixture onto one-half of the omelet and use a spatula to fold the empty side over the top. Slide the omelet onto a platter or cutting board.
7. To serve, cut the omelet in half and garnish with fresh parsley.

Nutrition:

Calories: 197
Fat: 18g
Protein: 6g

2. BANANA NUT OATMEAL

Preparation Time: 5 minutes

Cooking Time: 3 minutes

Servings: 1

Ingredients:

- Peeled banana
- ½ cup of skim milk
- ¼ cup of quick cooking oats
- 3 tbsp. of honey
- 2 tbsp. of chopped walnuts
- 1 tsp. of flax seeds

Directions:

1. In a microwave-safe dish, combine the milk, rice, sugar, walnuts, banana, and flax seeds.
2. Cook for 3 minutes in the oven, then mash the banana with a fork and whisk it into the mixture.
3. Serve and Enjoy!

Nutrition:

Calories: 344
Protein: 6.8g
Fat: 4.09g
Carbohydrates: 75.33g

3. MEDITERRANEAN TOFU SCRAMBLE

Preparation Time: 11 minutes

Cooking Time: 11 minutes

Servings: 4

Ingredients:

- 2 tbsp. of olive oil
- 1 diced purple onion
- 2 cloves of minced garlic
- 1 lb. of extra firm tofu
- 1 diced medium red bell pepper
- 1 tbsp. of lemon juice
- 2 tbsp. of soy sauce
- 2 tbsp. of seasoning
- 1 tsp. of ground turmeric
- ¼ cup of finely chopped fresh parsley
- chopped scallions
- ½ tsp. of red pepper flakes
- Toast
- Hot sauce pita bread hummus

Directions:

1. Place your big skillet over medium heat and coat the bottom with olive oil. Add the onion to the hot oil and cook until it has softened. It should only take about 5 minutes to complete. Cook for an extra minute after adding the garlic.
2. In a pan, crumble the tofu and add the soy sauce, bell pepper, seasoning, lemon juice, and red pepper flakes. Cook, tossing sometimes with a spatula, until the bell pepper bits are crisp and soft. It should only take about 5 minutes to complete. Remove the pan from the heat and add the scallions and parsley.

3. Serve with pita, toast, hot sauce, and hummus. Enjoy!

Nutrition:

Calories: 182
Protein: 12. 7g
Fat: 11. 16g
Carbohydrates: 10.1g

4. GREEK YOGURT WITH BERRIES AND SEEDS

Preparation Time: 3 minutes

Cooking Time: 0 minutes

Servings: 1

Ingredients:

- 1 handful of blueberries
- 1 handful of raspberries
- 1 tbsp. of greek yogurt
- 1 tsp. of sunflower seeds
- 1 tsp. of pumpkin seeds
- 1 tsp. of sliced almonds

Directions:

1. Wash and dry your berries. Place them into a dish.
2. Spoon your Greek yogurt on top and sprinkle it with your seeds and nuts.
3. Serve and enjoy!

Nutrition:

Calories: 127
Protein: 2.28g
Fat: 3.66g
Carbohydrates: 23.49g

5. SPINACH FRITTATA

Preparation Time: 15 minutes

Cooking Time: 20 minutes

Servings: 6

Ingredients:

- ¼ cup of kalamata olives, pitted and chopped.
- 8 eggs, beaten.
- 2 cups of spinach, chopped.
- 1 tbsp. of olive oil
- ½ tsp. of chili flakes
- 2 oz. feta cheese, crumbled.
- ¼ cup of plain yogurt

Directions:

1. Brush the pan with olive oil.
2. Mix up all the remaining ingredients in the mixing bowl.
3. Pour them into the pan.
4. Bake the frittata for 20 minutes at 355°F.
5. Serve.

Nutrition:

Calories: 145
Protein: 9.6g
Carbohydrates: 2.3g
Fat: 10.9g
Fiber: 0.4g

6. GARDEN SCRAMBLE

Preparation Time: 9 minutes

Cooking Time: 11 minutes

Servings: 2

Ingredients:

- 1 tsp. extra virgin olive oil
- ½ cup diced yellow squash
- ½ cup diced green bell pepper
- ¼ cup diced sweet white onion
- 6 cherry tomatoes, halved
- 1 tbsp. chopped fresh basil
- 1 tbsp. chopped fresh parsley
- ½ tsp. salt
- ¼ tsp. freshly ground black pepper
- 8 large eggs, beaten

Directions:

1. In a large nonstick skillet, cook olive oil over medium heat. Add the squash, pepper, and onion and sauté for 4 minutes.
2. Add the tomatoes, basil, and parsley and season. Sauté for 1 minute, then pour the beaten eggs over the vegetables. Close and reduce the heat to low.
3. Cook for 6 minutes, making sure the center is no longer runny.
4. To serve, slide the frittata onto a platter and cut into wedges.

Nutrition:

Calories: 211
Fat: 17g
Protein: 5g

7. SUMMER DAY FRUIT SALAD

Preparation Time: 16 minutes

Cooking Time: 0 minute

Servings: 2

Ingredients

- 2 cups honeydew melon cubes
- 2 cups red seedless grapes
- 1 cup sliced fresh strawberries
- 1 cup fresh blueberries
- Zest and juice of 1 large lime
- 2 cups cantaloupe cubes
- ½ cup unsweetened toasted coconut flakes
- ¼ cup honey
- ¼ tsp. salt
- ½ cup extra virgin olive oil

Directions:

1. Combine all the fruits, lime zest, and coconut flakes in a large bowl and stir well to blend. Set aside.
2. In a blender, mix lime juice, honey, and salt and blend on low. Once the honey is incorporated, slowly add the olive oil and blend until opaque.
3. Drizzle dressing over the fruit and mix well. Wrap and chill before serving.

Nutrition:

Calories: 196
Fat: 16g
Protein 3g

8. FRESH TOMATO PASTA BOWL

Preparation Time: 7 minutes

Cooking Time: 10 minutes

Servings: 2

Ingredients:

- 8-oz. whole-grain linguine
- 1 tbsp. extra virgin olive oil
- 2 garlic cloves, minced
- ¼ cup chopped yellow onion
- 1 tsp. chopped fresh oregano
- ½ tsp. salt
- ¼ tsp. freshly ground black pepper
- 1 tsp. tomato paste
- 8-oz. cherry tomatoes, halved
- ½ cup grated Parmesan cheese
- 1 tbsp. chopped fresh parsley

Directions:

1. Boil water at high heat and cook the linguine according to the package instructions until al dente. Set aside half cup of the pasta water. Do not rinse the pasta.
2. In a large, heavy skillet, heat the olive oil over medium-high heat. Sauté the garlic, onion, and oregano for 5 minutes.
3. Add the salt, pepper, tomato paste, and ¼ cup of the reserved pasta water. Stir well and cook for 1 minute.
4. Stir in the tomatoes and cooked pasta, tossing everything well to coat. Add more pasta water if needed.
5. To serve, top with Parmesan cheese and parsley.

Nutrition:

Calories: 391
Fat: 28g
Protein: 9g

9. BERRY BREAKFAST SMOOTHIE

Preparation Time: 3 minutes

Cooking Time: 0 minute

Servings: 2

Ingredients:

- ½ cup vanilla low-fat Greek yogurt
- ¼ cup low-fat milk
- ½ cup blueberries or strawberries
- 6 to 8 ice cubes

Directions:

1. Place the Greek yogurt, milk, and berries in a blender and blend until the berries are liquefied.
2. Mix in ice cubes and blend on high.
3. Serve immediately.

Nutrition:

Calories: 98
Fat: 10g
Protein: 7g

10. OAT AND FRUIT PARFAIT

Preparation Time: 11 minutes

Cooking Time: 10-12 minutes

Servings: 2

Ingredients:

- ½ cup whole-grain rolled oats
- ½ cup walnut pieces
- 1 tsp. honey
- 1 cup sliced fresh strawberries
- 1½ cups vanilla low-fat Greek yogurt
- Fresh mint leaves for garnish

Directions:

1. Preheat the oven to 300°F.
2. Spread the oats and walnuts in a single layer on a baking sheet.
3. Toast the oats and nuts just until you begin to smell the nuts, 10 to 12 minutes. Pull out the pan from the oven and set aside.
4. In a small microwave-safe bowl, heat the honey just until warm, about 30 seconds. Add the strawberries and stir to coat.
5. Place 1 tbsp. of the strawberries in the bottom of each of 2 dessert dishes or 8-oz. glasses. Add a portion of yogurt and then a portion of oats and repeat the layers until the containers are full, ending with the berries.
6. Serve.

Nutrition:

Calories: 108
Fat: 10g
Protein: 3g

11. PEACH SUNRISE SMOOTHIE

Preparation time: 6 minutes

Cooking Time: 0 minute

Servings: 2

Ingredients:

- 1 large unpeeled peach, pitted and sliced (about ½ cup)
- 6 oz. vanilla or peach low-fat Greek yogurt
- 2 tbsp. low-fat milk
- 6 to 8 ice cubes

Directions:

1. Incorporate all ingredients in a blender and blend until thick and creamy.
2. Serve immediately.

Nutrition:

Calories: 98
Fat: 16g
Protein: 3g

12. GARLICKY BROILED SARDINES

Preparation Time: 6 minutes

Cooking Time: 5 minutes

Servings: 2

Ingredients:

- 4 (3¼-oz.) cans sardines packed in water or olive oil
- 2 tbsp. extra virgin olive oil
- 4 garlic cloves, minced
- ½ tsp. red pepper flakes
- ½ tsp. salt
- ¼ tsp. black pepper

Directions:

1. Preheat the broiler. Line a baking dish with aluminum foil. Lay sardines in a single layer on the foil.
2. Combine the olive oil (if using), garlic, and red pepper flakes in a small bowl and spoon over each sardine. Season with salt and pepper.
3. Broil just until sizzling, 2 to 3 minutes.
4. To serve, place 4 sardines on each plate and top with any remaining garlic mixture that has collected in the baking dish.

Nutrition:

Calories: 308
Fat: 17g
Protein: 9g

13. EGG, PANCETTA, AND SPINACH BENEDICT

Preparation Time: 16 minutes

Cooking Time: 14-15 minutes

Servings: 2

Ingredients:

- ¼ cup diced pancetta
- 2 cups baby spinach leaves
- ¼ tsp. freshly ground black pepper
- ¼ tsp. salt, or to taste
- 2 large eggs
- Extra virgin olive oil (optional)
- 1 whole-grain English muffin, toasted

Directions:

1. In a medium, heavy skillet, brown the pancetta over medium-low heat for about 5 minutes, stirring frequently until crisp on all sides.
2. Stir in the spinach, pepper, and salt if desired (it may not need any, depending on how salty the pancetta is). Cook, stirring occasionally, for 5 minutes.
3. Transfer the mixture to a medium bowl.
4. Crack the eggs into the same pan (add olive oil if the pan looks dry) and cook until the whites are just opaque, 3 to 4 minutes. Carefully flip the eggs and continue cooking for 30 seconds to 1 minute until done to your preferred degree for over-easy eggs.
5. Situate muffin half on each of 2 plates and top each with half of the spinach mixture and 1 egg, yolk side up. Pierce the yolks just before serving.

Nutrition:

Calories: 391
Fat: 21g
Protein: 15g

14. CHEESY STUFFED TOMATOES

Preparation Time: 6 minutes

Cooking Time: 20-25 minutes

Servings: 2

Ingredients:

- 4 large, ripe tomatoes
- 1 tbsp. extra virgin olive oil
- 2 garlic cloves, minced
- ½ cup diced yellow onion
- ½ lb. cremini mushrooms
- 1 tbsp. chopped fresh basil
- 1 tbsp. chopped fresh oregano
- ½ tsp. salt
- ¼ tsp. freshly ground black pepper
- 1 cup shredded part-skim mozzarella cheese
- 1 tbsp. grated Parmesan cheese

Directions:

1. Preheat the oven to 375°F. Line a baking sheet with aluminum foil.
2. Cut sliver from the bottom of each tomato so they will stand upright without wobbling.
3. Cut a ½-inch slice from the top of each tomato and use a spoon to gently remove most of the pulp, placing it in a medium bowl.
4. Place the tomatoes on the baking sheet.
5. In a skillet, cook olive oil over medium heat. Sauté the garlic, onion, mushrooms, basil, and oregano for 5 minutes and season with salt and pepper.
6. Transfer the mixture to the bowl and blend well with the tomato pulp. Stir in the mozzarella cheese.

7. Fill each tomato loosely with the mixture, top with Parmesan cheese, and bake until the cheese is bubbly, 15 to 20 minutes. Serve immediately.

Nutrition:

Calories: 201
Fat: 19g
Protein: 6g

15. SAVORY AVOCADO SPREAD

Preparation Time: 17 minutes

Cooking Time: 0 minute

Servings: 2

Ingredients:

- 1 ripe avocado
- 1 tsp. lemon juice
- 6 boneless sardine filets
- ¼ cup diced sweet white onion
- 1 stalk celery, diced
- ½ tsp. salt
- ¼ tsp. black pepper

Directions:

1. In a blender, pulse avocado, lemon juice, and sardine filets.
2. Ladle the mixture into a small bowl and stir in the onion, celery, salt, and pepper. Mix well with a fork and serve as desired.

Nutrition:

Calories: 109
Fat: 15g
Protein: 6g

16. EGGS AND GREENS BREAKFAST DISH

Preparation Time: 8 minutes

Cooking Time: 10-12 minutes

Serving 2

Ingredients

- 1 tbsp. of olive oil
- 2 cups of chopped and steamed rainbow chard
- 1 cup of fresh spinach
- 1/2 cup of arugula
- 2 cloves of garlic, minced
- 4 pounded eggs
- 1/2 cup sliced Cheddar cheese
- To taste: salt or black pepper

Directions:

1. Heat oil over medium-high heat in a skillet. Sauté the spinach, chard, and arugula for around 3 minutes until tender.
2. Add garlic; cook and mix for around 2 minutes until fragrant.
3. In a cup, mix the eggs and cheese; pour in the chard mix. Cover and cook for 5 to 7 minutes until set.
4. Season with pepper and salt.

Nutrition:

Calories: 333
Fat: 26.2g
Carbs: 4.2g
Protein: 21g

17. HEART-HEALTHFUL TRAIL MIX

Preparation Time: 8 minutes

Cooking Time: 32 minutes

Servings: 2

Ingredients:

- 1 cup raw almonds
- 1 cup walnut halves
- 1 cup pumpkin seeds
- 1 cup dried apricots, cut into thin strips
- 1 cup dried cherries, roughly chopped
- 1 cup golden raisins
- 2 tbsp. extra virgin olive oil
- 1 tsp. salt

Directions:

1. Preheat the oven to 300°F. Line a baking sheet with aluminum foil.
2. In a large bowl, mix almonds, walnuts, pumpkin seeds, apricots, cherries, and raisins. Pour the olive oil over all and toss well with clean hands. Add salt and toss again to distribute.
3. Fill in the nut mixture onto the baking sheet in a single layer and bake until the fruits begin to brown, about 30 minutes.
4. Chill on the baking sheet to room temperature.
5. Store in a large, airtight container or Ziploc plastic bag.

Nutrition:

Calories: 109
Fat: 7g
Protein: 1g

18. CITRUS-KISSED MELON

Preparation Time: 11 minutes

Cooking Time: 0 minute

Servings: 2

Ingredients:

- 2 cups cubed melon
- 2 cups cubed cantaloupe
- ½ cup freshly squeezed orange juice
- ¼ cup freshly squeezed lime juice
- 1 tbsp. orange zest

Directions:

1. In a large bowl, incorporate melon cubes. In a bowl, blend the orange juice, lime juice, and orange zest and pour over the fruit.
2. Cover and let cool, stirring occasionally. Serve chilled.

Nutrition:

Calories: 101
Fat: 11g
Protein: 2g

19. AVOCADO EGG SCRAMBLE

Preparation Time: 8 minutes

Cooking Time: 15 minutes

Servings: 2

Ingredients

- 4 eggs, beaten
- 1 white onion, diced
- 1 tbsp. avocado oil
- 1 avocado, finely chopped
- ½ tsp. chili flakes
- 1 oz. cheddar cheese, shredded
- ½ tsp. salt
- 1 tbsp. fresh parsley

Directions:

1. Pour avocado oil in the skillet and bring it to boil.
2. Add diced onion and roast until it is light brown.
3. Mix up together chili flakes, beaten eggs, and salt.
4. Pour the egg mixture over the cooked onion and cook the mixture for 1 minute over medium heat.
5. Scramble the eggs well with the help of the fork or spatula. Cook the eggs until they are solid but soft.
6. Add chopped avocado and shredded cheese.
7. Stir the scramble well and transfer to the serving plates.
8. Sprinkle the meal with fresh parsley.

Nutrition:

Calories: 236
Fat: 20g

Protein: 8.6g

20. CAFÉ COOLER

Preparation Time: 16 minutes

Cooking time: 0 minute

Servings: 2

Ingredients:

- Ice cubes
- 2 cups low-fat milk
- ½ tsp. ground cinnamon
- ½ tsp. pure vanilla extract
- 1 cup espresso, cooled to room temperature
- 4 tsp. sugar (optional)

Directions:

1. Fill four tall glasses with ice cubes.
2. In a blender, combine the milk, cinnamon, and vanilla and blend until frothy.
3. Pour the milk over the ice cubes and top each drink with ¼ of the espresso. If using sugar, stir it into the espresso until it dissolves.
4. Serve immediately with chilled teaspoon for stirring.

Nutrition:

Calories: 93
Fat: 7g
Protein: 1g

CHAPTER SEVEN

STEW AND SOUP RECIPES

21. CREAMY CAULIFLOWER SOUP

Preparation Time: 15 minutes

Cooking Time: 30 minutes

Servings: 6

Ingredients:

- 5 cups cauliflower rice
- 8 oz. cheddar cheese, grated
- 2 cups unsweetened almond milk
- 2 cups vegetable stock
- 2 tbsp. water
- 1 small onion, chopped
- 2 garlic cloves, minced
- 1 tbsp. olive oil
- Pepper
- Salt

Directions:

1. Cook olive oil in a large stockpot over medium heat.

2. Add onion and garlic and cook for 1-2 minutes. Add cauliflower rice and water.
3. Cover and cook for 5-7 minutes.
4. Add vegetable stock and almond milk and stir well.
5. Bring to boil.
6. Turn heat to low and simmer for 5 minutes.
7. Turn off the heat.
8. Slowly add cheddar cheese and stir until smooth.
9. Season soup with pepper and salt.
10. Stir well and serve hot.

Nutrition:

Calories 214
Fat: 16.5g
Protein: 11.6g

22. TOFU STIR FRY WITH ASPARAGUS

Preparation Time: 15 minutes

Cooking Time: 21 minutes

Servings: 4

Ingredients:

- 1 lb. asparagus, cut off stems
- 2 tbsp. olive oil
- 2 blocks tofu, pressed and cubed
- 2 garlic cloves, minced
- 1 tsp. Cajun spice mix
- 1 tsp. mustard
- 1 bell pepper, chopped
- ¼ cup vegetable broth
- Salt and black pepper, to taste

Directions:

1. Using a huge saucepan with lightly salted water, place in asparagus and cook until tender for 10 minutes; drain.
2. Set a wok over high heat and warm olive oil; stir in tofu cubes and cook for 6 minutes.
3. Place in garlic and cook for 30 seconds until soft.
4. Stir in the remaining ingredients, including reserved asparagus, cook for an additional 4 minutes.
5. Divide among plates and serve.

Nutrition:

Calories: 138
Fat: 8.9g
Protein: 6.4g

23. CREAM OF THYME TOMATO SOUP

Preparation Time: 5 minutes

Cooking Time: 20 minutes

Servings: 6

Ingredients:

- 2 tbsp. ghee
- 2 large red onions, diced
- ½ cup raw cashew nuts, diced
- 2 (28 oz.) cans tomatoes
- 1 tsp. fresh thyme leaves + extra to garnish
- 1 ½ cups water
- Salt and black pepper to taste

Directions:

1. Cook ghee in a pot over medium heat and sauté the onions for 4 minutes until softened.
2. Stir in the tomatoes, thyme, water, cashews, and season with salt and black pepper.
3. Cover and bring to simmer for 10 minutes until thoroughly cooked.
4. Open, turn the heat off, and puree the ingredients with an immersion blender.
5. Adjust to taste and stir in the heavy cream.
6. Spoon into soup bowls and serve.

Nutrition:

Calories: 310
Fat: 27g
Protein: 11g

24. LIME-MINT SOUP

Preparation Time: 5 minutes

Cooking Time: 20 minutes

Servings: 4

Ingredients:

- 4 cups vegetable broth
- ¼ cup fresh mint leaves
- ¼ cup scallions
- 3 garlic cloves, minced
- 3 tbsp. freshly squeezed lime juice

Directions:

1. In a large stockpot, combine the broth, mint, scallions, garlic, and lime juice.
2. Bring to a boil over medium-high heat.
3. Cover, set heat to low, simmer for 15 minutes, and serve.

Nutrition:

Calories: 214
Fat: 2g
Protein: 5g

25. ASPARAGUS AVOCADO SOUP

Preparation Time: 10 minutes

Cooking Time: 20 minutes

Servings: 4

Ingredients:

- 1 avocado, peeled, pitted, cubed
- 12 oz. asparagus
- ½ tsp. ground black pepper
- 1 tsp. garlic powder
- 1 tsp. sea salt
- 2 tbsp. olive oil, divided
- ½ lemon, juiced
- 2 cups vegetable stock

Directions:

1. Switch on the air fryer, insert fryer basket, grease it with olive oil, then shut with its lid, set the fryer at 425°F, and preheat for 5 minutes.
2. Place asparagus in a shallow dish, drizzle with 1 tbsp. oil, sprinkle with garlic powder, salt, and black pepper, and toss until well-mixed.
3. Open the fryer, add asparagus, close with a lid, and cook for 10 minutes until nicely golden and roasted, shaking halfway through the frying.
4. When the air fryer beeps, open the lid and transfer asparagus to a food processor.
5. Add remaining ingredients into a food processor and pulse until well-combined and smooth.

6. Tip the soup in a saucepan, pour in water if the soup is too thick, and heat it over medium-low heat for 5 minutes until thoroughly heated.
7. Ladle soup into bowls and serve.

Nutrition:

Calories: 208
Fat: 11g
Protein: 4g

26. SPINACH AND ORZO SOUP

Preparation Time: 10 minutes

Cooking Time: 10 minutes

Servings: 4

Ingredients:

- ½ cup orzo
- 6 cups chicken soup
- 1½ cups Parmesan cheese, grated
- Salt and black pepper to taste
- 1½ tsp. oregano, dried
- ¼ cup yellow onion, finely chopped
- 3 cups baby spinach
- 2 tbsp. lemon juice
- ½ cup peas, frozen

Directions:

1. Heat a saucepan with the stock over high heat, add oregano, orzo, onion, salt, and pepper, stir, bring to a boil, cover, and cook for 10 minutes.
2. Take soup off the heat, add salt and pepper to taste, and the rest of the ingredients.
3. Stir well and divide into soup bowls. Serve right away.

Nutrition:

Calories: 201
Fat: 5g
Fiber: 3g
Carbs: 28g
Protein: 17g

27. MINTY LENTIL AND SPINACH SOUP

Preparation Time: 10 minutes

Cooking Time: 31 minutes

Servings: 6

Ingredients:

- 2 tbsp. olive oil
- 1 yellow onion, chopped
- A pinch of salt and black pepper
- 2 garlic cloves, minced
- 1 tsp. coriander, ground
- 1 tsp. cumin, ground
- 1 tsp. sumac
- 1 tsp. red pepper, crushed
- 2 tsp. mint, dried
- 1 tbsp. flour
- 6 cups veggie stock
- 3 cups water
- 12 oz. spinach, torn
- 1½ cups brown lentils, rinsed
- 2 cups parsley, chopped
- Juice of 1 lime

Directions:

1. Heat up a pot with the oil over medium heat, add onions, stir and sauté for 5 minutes.
2. Add garlic, salt, pepper, coriander, cumin, sumac, red pepper, mint, and flour, stir and cook for another minute.
3. Add the stock, water, and the other ingredients except the parsley and lime juice, stir, bring to a simmer, and cook for 20 minutes.

4. Add the parsley and lime juice, cook the soup for 5 minutes more, ladle into bowls, and serve.

Nutrition:

Calories: 170
Fat: 7g
Fiber: 6g
Carbs: 22g
Protein: 8g

28. SHRIMP SOUP

Preparation Time: 30 minutes

Cooking Time: 3 minutes

Servings: 6

Ingredients:

- 1 English cucumber, chopped
- 3 cups tomato juice
- 3 jarred roasted red peppers, chopped
- ½ cup olive oil
- 2 tbsp. sherry vinegar
- 1 tsp. sherry vinegar
- 1 garlic clove, mashed
- 2 baguette slices, cut into cubes and toasted
- Salt and black pepper to taste
- ½ tsp. cumin, ground
- ¾ pound of shrimp, peeled and deveined
- 1 tsp. thyme, chopped

Directions:

1. In a blender, mix cucumber with tomato juice, red peppers and pulse well.
2. Add bread, 6 tbsp. oil, 2 tbsp. vinegar, cumin, salt, pepper, and garlic, pulse again.
3. Transfer to a bowl and keep in the fridge for 30 minutes.
4. Heat a saucepan with 1 tbsp. oil over high heat, add shrimp, stir and cook for 2 minutes.
5. Add thyme and the rest of the ingredients, cook for 1 minute and transfer to a plate.
6. Divide cold soup into bowls, top with shrimp, and serve. Enjoy!

Nutrition:

Calories: 230
Fat: 7g
Fiber: 10g
Carbs: 24g
Protein: 13g

29. CUCUMBER SOUP

Preparation Time: 10 minutes

Cooking Time: 6 minutes

Servings: 4

Ingredients:

- 3 bread slices
- ¼ cup almonds
- 4 tsp. almonds
- 3 cucumbers, peeled and chopped
- 3 garlic cloves, minced
- ½ cup warm water
- 6 scallions, thinly sliced
- ¼ cup white wine vinegar
- 3 tbsp. olive oil
- Salt to taste
- 1 tsp. lemon juice
- ½ cup green grapes, cut in halves

Directions:

1. Heat a pan over medium-high heat, add almonds, stir, toast for 5 minutes, transfer to a plate, and leave aside.
2. Soak bread in warm water for 2 minutes, transfer to a blender, add almost all the cucumber, salt, oil, garlic, 5 scallions, lemon juice, vinegar, and half of the almonds. Pulse well.
3. Ladle soup into bowls, top with reserved ingredients and 2 tbsp. grapes, and serve.

Nutrition:

Calories: 200
Fat: 12g

Fiber: 3g
Carbs: 20g
Protein: 6g

30. CHICKPEAS, TOMATO, AND KALE STEW

Preparation Time: 10 minutes

Cooking Time: 30 minutes

Servings: 4

Ingredients:

- 1 yellow onion, chopped
- 1 tbsp. extra virgin olive oil
- 2 cups sweet potatoes, peeled and chopped
- 1½ tsp. cumin, ground
- 4-inch cinnamon stick
- 14 oz. canned tomatoes, chopped
- 14 oz. canned chickpeas, drained
- 1½ tsp. honey
- 6 tbsp. orange juice
- 1 cup water
- Salt and black pepper to taste
- ½ cup green olives, pitted
- 2 cups kale leaves, chopped

Directions:

1. Heat a saucepan with the oil over medium high heat, add onion, cumin, and cinnamon, stir and cook for 5 minutes.
2. Add potatoes and the rest of the ingredients except the kale. Stir, cover, reduce heat to medium-low, and cook for 15 minutes.
3. Add kale, stir, cover again, and cook for 10 more minutes. Divide into bowls and serve.

Nutrition:

Calories: 280
Fat: 6g

Fiber: 9g
Carbs: 53g
Protein: 10g

31. TOMATO BASIL SOUP

Preparation Time: 10 minutes

Cooking Time: 10 minutes

Servings: 2

Ingredients:

- 1 cup tomatoes, chopped
- ½ cup water
- 1 cup basil leaves
- 1 tbsp. low-sodium and low-fat cheese, shredded

Directions:

1. Place the tomatoes in a saucepan. Pour water. Close the lid.
2. Set heat to medium and allow the tomatoes to boil.
3. Using a handheld blender, puree the tomatoes while still in a pan.
4. Add in the basil leaves and allow to cook for another 2 minutes.
5. Scoop in bowls and serve with ½ tbsp. each shredded cheese.

Nutrition:

Calories: 137
Fat: 2g
Protein: 6g

32. CREAMY BROCCOLI SOUP

Preparation Time: 10 minutes

Cooking Time: 35 minutes

Servings: 2

Ingredients:

- 20 oz. frozen broccoli, thawed and chopped
- ¼ tsp. nutmeg
- 4 cups vegetable broth
- 1 potato, peeled and chopped
- 2 garlic cloves, peeled and chopped
- 1 large onion, chopped
- 1 tbsp. olive oil
- Pepper
- Salt

Directions:

1. Cook oil in a large saucepan at medium heat.
2. Add garlic and onion and sauté until onion is tender.
3. Add potato, broccoli, and broth and bring to boil. Turn heat to low and simmer for 15 minutes or until vegetables are tender.
4. Using a blender, puree the soup until smooth. Season soup with nutmeg, pepper, and salt.

Nutrition:

Calories: 184
Fat: 6g
Protein: 21g

33. SHRIMP & ARUGULA SOUP

Preparation Time: 5 minutes

Cooking Time: 32 minutes

Servings: 2

Ingredients:

- 10 medium-sized shrimp or 5 large prawns, cleaned, deshelled, and deveined
- 1 small red onion, sliced very thinly
- 1 cup arugula
- 1 cup baby kale
- 2 large celery stalks, sliced very thinly
- 5 sprigs of parsley, chopped
- 11 cloves of garlic, minced
- 5 cups of chicken or fish or vegetable stock
- 1 tbsp. extra virgin olive oil
- Dash of sea salt
- Dash of pepper

Directions:

1. Sauté the vegetables (not the kale or arugula yet), in a stockpot on low heat for about 2 minutes, so that they are still tender and crunchy, but not cooked quite yet.
2. Add the salt and pepper.
3. Clean and chop the shrimp into bite-sized pieces that would be comfortable eating in a soup.
4. Add the shrimp to the pot and sauté for 10 minutes on medium-low heat.
5. Make sure the shrimp is cooked thoroughly and not translucent.
6. When the shrimp seems to be cooked through, add the stock to the pot and cook on medium for about 20 minutes.

7. Remove from heat and cool before serving.

Nutrition:

Calories: 254
Fat: 2g
Protein: 33g

34. CREAMY CHICKEN SOUP

Preparation Time: 10 minutes

Cooking Time: 30 minutes

Servings: 2

Ingredients:

- 4 chicken breasts
- 1 carrot, chopped
- 1 cup zucchini, peeled and chopped
- 2 cups cauliflower, broken into florets
- 1 celery rib, chopped
- 1 small onion, chopped
- 5 cups water
- ½ tsp. salt
- Black pepper, to taste

Directions:

1. Place chicken breasts, onion, carrot, celery, cauliflower, and zucchini in a deep soup pot.
2. Add in salt, black pepper, and 5 cups of water.
3. Stir and bring to a boil.
4. Simmer for 30 minutes, then remove chicken from the pot and let it cool slightly.
5. Blend the soup until completely smooth.
6. Shred or dice the chicken meat, return it back to the pot, stir, and serve.

Nutrition:

Calories: 190
Fat: 2g
Protein: 6g

35. BROCCOLI AND CHICKEN SOUP

Preparation Time: 5 minutes

Cooking Time: 34-36 minutes

Servings: 2

Ingredients:

- 4 boneless chicken thighs, diced
- 1 small carrot, chopped
- 1 broccoli head, broken into florets
- 1 garlic clove, chopped
- 1 small onion, chopped
- 4 cups water
- 3 tbsp. extra virgin olive oil
- ½ tsp. salt
- Black pepper, to taste

Directions:

1. Using a deep soup pot, cook olive oil and gently sauté broccoli for 2-3 minutes, stirring occasionally.
2. Add in onion, carrot, chicken, and cook, stirring, for 2-3 minutes. Stir in salt, black pepper, and water.
3. Bring to a boil. Simmer for 30 minutes, then remove from heat and set aside to cool.
4. In a blender, process the soup until completely smooth.

Nutrition:

Calories: 185
Fat: 2g
Protein: 22g

CHAPTER EIGHT

POULTRY RECIPES

36. CHICKEN SKILLET

Preparation time: 10 minutes

Cooking time: 35 minutes

Servings: 6

Ingredients:

- 6 chicken thighs, bone-in and skin-on
- Juice of 2 lemons
- 1 tsp. oregano, dried
- 1 red onion, chopped
- Salt and black pepper to the taste
- 1 tsp. garlic powder
- 2 garlic cloves, minced
- 2 tbsp. olive oil
- 2½ cups chicken stock
- 1 cup white rice
- 1 tbsp. oregano, chopped
- 1 cup green olives, pitted and sliced
- ⅓ cup parsley, chopped
- ½ cup feta cheese, crumbled

Directions:

1. Heat up a pan with the oil over medium heat, add the chicken thighs skin side down, cook for 4 minutes on each side, and transfer to a plate.
2. Add the garlic and onion to the pan, stir and sauté for 5 minutes.
3. Add the rice, salt, pepper, stock, oregano, and lemon juice, stir, cook for 1-2 minutes more, and take off the heat.
4. Add the chicken to the pan, place the pan in the oven, and bake at 375°F for 25 minutes.
5. Add the cheese, olives, and parsley, divide the whole mix between plates, and serve for lunch.

Nutrition:

Calories: 432
Fat: 18.5g
Fiber: 13.6g
Carbs: 27.8g
Protein: 25.6g

37. CHICKEN STUFFED PEPPERS

Preparation time: 10 minutes

Cooking time: 0 minutes

Servings: 6

Ingredients:

- 1 cup Greek yogurt
- 2 tbsp. mustard
- Salt and black pepper to the taste
- 1 lb. rotisserie chicken meat, cubed
- 4 celery stalks, chopped
- 2 tbsp. balsamic vinegar
- 1 bunch scallions, sliced
- ¼ cup parsley, chopped
- 1 cucumber, sliced
- 3 red bell peppers, halved and deseeded
- 1 pint cherry tomatoes, quartered

Directions:

1. In a bowl, mix the chicken with the celery and rest of the ingredients except the bell peppers and toss well.
2. Stuff the pepper halves with the chicken mix and serve for lunch.

Nutrition:

Calories: 266
Fat: 12.2g
Fiber: 4.5g
Carbs: 15.7g
Protein: 3.7g

38. CHICKEN SHAWARMA

Preparation Time: 8 minutes

Cooking Time: 15 minutes

Servings: 8

Ingredients:

- 2 lb. chicken breast, sliced into strips
- 1 tsp. paprika
- 1 tsp. ground cumin
- ¼ tsp. granulated garlic
- ½ tsp. turmeric
- ¼ tsp. ground allspice

Directions

1. Season the chicken with the spices and a little salt and pepper.
2. Pour 1 cup chicken broth on the skillet.
3. Seal the skillet.
4. Choose the poultry setting.
5. Cook for 15 minutes.
6. Release the pressure naturally. Serve with flatbread.

Nutrition:

Calories: 481
Fat: 21g
Protein: 9g

39. TURKEY AND ASPARAGUS MIX

Preparation time: 10 minutes

Cooking time: 29 minutes

Servings: 4

Ingredients:

- 1 bunch asparagus, trimmed and halved
- 1 big turkey breast, skinless, boneless, and cut into strips
- 1 tsp. basil, dried
- 2 tbsp. olive oil
- A pinch of salt and black pepper
- ½ cup tomato sauce
- 1 tbsp. chives, chopped

Directions:

1. Heat up a pan with the oil over medium-high heat, add the turkey and brown for 4 minutes.
2. Add the asparagus and rest of the ingredients except the chives, bring to a simmer, and cook over medium heat for 25 minutes.
3. Add the chives, divide the mix between plates, and serve.

Nutrition:

Calories: 337
Fat: 21. 2g
Fiber: 10.2g
Carbs: 21.4g
Protein: 17.6g

40. YOGURT CHICKEN AND RED ONION MIX

Preparation time: 10 minutes

Cooking time: 30 minutes

Servings: 4

Ingredients:

- 2 pound chicken breast, skinless, boneless and sliced
- 3 tbsp. olive oil
- ¼ cup Greek yogurt
- 2 garlic cloves, minced
- ½ tsp. onion powder
- A pinch of salt and black pepper
- 4 red onions, sliced

Directions:

1. In a roasting pan, combine the chicken with the oil, yogurt, and other ingredients, place in the oven at 375°F, and bake for 30 minutes.
2. Divide chicken mix between plates and serve hot.

Nutrition:

Calories: 278
Fat: 15g
Fiber: 9.2g
Carbs: 15.1g
Protein: 23.3g

41. CHICKEN WITH GREEK SALAD

Prep time: 25 minutes

Cook time: 0 minutes

Serving 4

Ingredients

- 2 tbsp. extra virgin olive oil
- ⅓ cup red-wine vinegar
- 1 tsp. garlic powder
- 1 tbsp. chopped fresh dill
- ¼ tsp. sea salt
- ¼ tsp. freshly ground pepper
- 2½ cups chopped cooked chicken
- 6 cups chopped romaine lettuce
- 1 cucumber, peeled, seeded, and chopped
- 2 medium tomatoes, chopped
- ½ cup crumbled feta cheese
- ½ cup sliced ripe black olives
- ½ cup finely chopped red onion

Directions:

1. Whisk the extra virgin olive oil, vinegar, garlic powder, dill, sea salt, and pepper together in a large cup.
2. To combine well, add the chicken, lettuce, cucumber, tomatoes, feta, and olives, then toss. Enjoy!

Nutrition:

Calories: 337
Fat: 21.2g
Fiber: 10.2g
Carbs: 21.4g

Protein: 17.6g

42. BRAISED CHICKEN WITH MUSHROOMS AND OLIVES

Prep time: 10 minutes

Cook time: 33 minutes

Servings 4

Ingredients

- 2½ pounds chicken, cut into pieces
- Sea salt
- Freshly ground pepper
- 1 tbsp. plus
- 1 tsp. extra virgin olive oil
- 16 cloves garlic, peeled
- 10 oz. cremini mushrooms, rinsed, trimmed, and halved
- ½ cup white wine
- ⅓ cup chicken stock
- ½ cup green olives pitted

Directions:

1. Over medium-high heat, prepare a large skillet.
2. Meanwhile, the chicken should be seasoned with sea salt and pepper.
3. To the heated skillet, add 1 tbsp. of extra virgin olive oil and add the chicken, skin side down; cook for around 6 minutes or until browned.
4. Move it to a dish and set it aside.
5. Add 1 tsp. of the remaining extra virgin olive oil to the pan and sauté for around 6 minutes or until the garlic and mushrooms are browned.
6. Add the wine and bring to a boil, reduce the heat, and cook for approximately 1 minute.

7. Send the chicken back to the pan and stir in the olives and chicken broth.
8. Return the mixture to a gentle boil, reduce heat and cook, covered, for about 20 minutes or until the chicken is thoroughly cooked.

Nutrition:

Calories: 437
Fat: 23.2g
Fiber: 11.2g
Carbs: 31.2g
Protein: 15.6g

43. CHICKEN WITH OLIVES, MUSTARD GREENS, AND LEMON

Prep time: 10 minutes

Cook time: 30 minutes

Servings 6

Ingredients

- 2 tbsp. extra virgin olive oil, divided
- 6 skinless chicken breast halves, cut in half crosswise
- ½ cup Kalamata olives pitted
- 1 tbsp. freshly squeezed lemon juice
- 1½ pound mustard greens, stalks removed and coarsely chopped
- 1 cup dry white wine
- 4 garlic cloves, smashed
- 1 medium red onion, halved and thinly sliced
- Sea salt
- Ground pepper
- Lemon wedges, for serving

Directions:

1. In a Dutch oven or large, heavy pot, heat 1 tbsp. of extra virgin olive oil over medium heat.
2. Rub the chicken with sea salt and pepper and add half of it to the mixing bowl; cook on all sides for about 8 minutes or until browned.
3. Switch to a plate with the cooked chicken and repeat with the remaining chicken and oil.
4. Add the garlic and onion to the pot and heat to medium; cook, stirring until tender, or for about 6 minutes.
5. Add the chicken and wine (with accumulated juices) and bring it to a boil.

6. Reduce the heat and cook for approximately 5 minutes, sealed.
7. On top of the chicken, add the greens and sprinkle it with sea salt and pepper.
8. Cook for 5 more minutes or until the greens are wilted and chicken is opaque.
9. Stir in the olives and lemon juice and remove the pot from the heat.
10. Serve drizzled and garnished with lemon wedges and collected pan juices.

Nutrition:

Calories: 336
Fat: 20.2g
Fiber: 12.2g
Carbs: 22.4g
Protein: 17.6g

44. WARM CHICKEN AVOCADO SALAD

Prep time: 15 minutes

Cook time: 15 minutes

Servings 4

Ingredients

- 2 tbsp. extra virgin olive oil, divided
- 500g chicken breast fillets
- 1 large avocado, peeled, diced
- 2 garlic cloves, sliced
- 1 tsp. ground turmeric
- 3 tsp. ground cumin
- 1 small head broccoli, chopped
- 1 large carrot, diced
- ⅓ cup currants
- 1½ cups chicken stock
- 1½ cups couscous
- Pinch of sea salt

Directions:

1. Heat 1 tbsp. of extra virgin olive oil in a large frying pan set over medium heat; add chicken and cook for about 6 minutes on each side or until cooked through; move to a plate and keep warm.
2. Meanwhile, in a heatproof dish, mix the currants and couscous; stir in the boiling stock and set aside, covered, for at least 5 minutes or until the liquid has been absorbed.
3. Separate the grains with a fork.
4. In a frying pan, add the remaining oil and add the carrots; cook for about 1 minute, stirring.
5. For about 1 minute, stir in the broccoli; add the garlic, turmeric, and cumin.

6. Cook for another 1 minute or so, then remove the pan from the oven.
7. Break the chicken into small slices and add to the mixture of broccoli, toss to combine, season with sea salt, and serve with the sprinkled avocado on top.

Nutrition:

Calories: 327
Fat: 21.2g
Fiber: 13.2g
Carbs: 20.4g
Protein 17.6g

45. CORONATION CHICKEN SALAD SIRTFOOD

Preparation Time: 2 minutes

Cooking Time: 2 minutes

Servings: 1

Ingredients:

- 75 g natural yogurt
- 1 tsp. coriander, chopped
- Juice of ¼ of a lemon
- ½ tsp. mild curry powder
- 1 tsp. ground turmeric
- Walnut halves, finely chopped
- 100g cooked chicken breast, cut into bite-sized pieces
- 20g red onion, diced
- 1 bird's eye chili
- 1 medjool date, finely chopped
- 40g rocket, to serve

Directions:

1. Take a bowl, gather the ingredients, and mix them in a bowl
2. Serve the salad on the rocket bedding.

Nutrition:

Calories: 364
Carbs: 45g
Fat: 12g
Protein: 15g

46. MOROCCAN CHICKEN CASSEROLE

Preparation Time: 5 minutes

Cooking Time: 35 minutes

Servings: 3

Ingredients:

- 250g (9oz) tinned chickpeas (garbanzo beans) drained
- Chicken breasts, cubed
- Medjool dates halved
- Dried apricots, halved
- 1 red onion, sliced
- 1 carrot, chopped
- 1 tsp ground cumin
- 1 tsp ground cinnamon
- 1 tsp ground turmeric
- 1 bird's eye chili, chopped
- 600ml (1 pint) chicken stock (broth)
- 25g (1oz) corn flour
- 60ml (2fl oz.) water
- 1 tbsp. fresh coriander

Directions:

1. Place the chicken, chickpeas (garbanzo beans), onion, carrot, chili, cumin, turmeric, cinnamon, and stock (broth) into a large saucepan.
2. Bring it to the boil, reduce the heat, and simmer for 25 minutes.
3. Add in the dates and apricots and simmer for 10 minutes.
4. In a cup, mix the corn flour with the water until it becomes a smooth paste.
5. Pour the mixture into the saucepan and stir until it thickens.
6. Add in the coriander (cilantro) and mix well.

Nutrition:

Calories: 423
Fat: 12g
Carbohydrates: 0g
Protein: 39g
Fiber: 0g

47. CHICKEN AND LEEKS PAN

Preparation time: 10 minutes

Cooking time: 20 minutes

Servings: 4

Ingredients:

- 2 tbsp. olive oil
- 1 lb. chicken breast, skinless, boneless, and cut into strips
- shallots, chopped
- 1 cup mozzarella cheese, shredded
- 2 leeks, sliced
- ½ cup veggie stock
- 1 tbsp. heavy cream
- 1 tsp. sweet paprika
- Salt and black pepper to the taste

Directions:

1. Ensure you heat the pan, add the shallots, stir, then cook for 3 minutes.
2. Add the meat and leeks, stir and brown for 7 minutes more.
3. Add the other ingredients except the cheese and stir.
4. Sprinkle the cheese on top, place the pan into the oven, then cook everything at 400°F for 10 minutes more.
5. Divide the mix between plates and serve.

Nutrition:

Calories: 253
Fat: 12.9g
Fiber: 1g
Carbs: 7.2g
Protein: 26.9g

48. CHICKEN AND PEPPERS MIX

Preparation time: 10 minutes

Cooking time: 25 minutes

Servings: 4

Ingredients:

- 1 cup red bell peppers, cut into strips
- 1 lb. chicken breast, skinless, boneless, and roughly cubed
- spring onions, chopped
- 2 tbsp. olive oil
- 1 tomato, cubed
- Salt and black pepper to the taste
- ¼ cup tomato passata
- 1 tbsp. cilantro, chopped

Directions:

1. Ensure you heat the pan, add the spring onions, and sauté them for 2 minutes.
2. Add the chicken and bell peppers, stir, then cook everything for 8 minutes more.
3. Add the rest of the ingredients, bring to a simmer, then cook over medium heat for 15 minutes more, stirring often.
4. Divide the mix between plates and serve

Nutrition:

Calories: 206
Fat: 10g
Fiber: 0.9g
Carbs: 3.7g
Protein: 24.8g

49. PAPRIKA CHICKEN MIX

Preparation time: 10 minutes

Cooking time: 22 minutes

Servings: 4

Ingredients:

- 1 cup mozzarella, shredded
- 2 tbsp. olive oil
- Shallots, chopped
- 1 lb. chicken breast, skinless, boneless and roughly cubed
- Salt and black pepper to the taste
- 1 cup carrots, sliced
- 1 tsp. sweet paprika
- ¼ tsp. onion powder
- ¼ tsp. garlic powder
- ½ cup chicken stock
- 1 tbsp. chives, chopped

Directions:

1. Ensure you heat the pan; add the shallots and sauté for 2 minutes.
2. Add the carrots, paprika, onion, and garlic powder; stir and sauté for 3 minutes.
3. Add the meat and brown it for 5 minutes.
4. Add the stock, sprinkle the cheese, and then cook everything for 15 minutes.
5. Sprinkle the chives on top, divide the mix between plates, and serve.

Nutrition:

Calories: 200
Fat: 4.5g

Fiber: 3.5g
Carbs: 8.5g
Protein: 10g

50. HONEY BALSAMIC CHICKEN

Preparation Time: 7 minutes

Cooking Time: 40 minutes

Servings: 5

Ingredients:

- ¼ cup honey
- ½ cup balsamic vinegar
- ¼ cup soy sauce
- 2 cloves garlic minced
- 10 chicken drumsticks

Directions

1. Mix the honey, vinegar, soy sauce, and garlic in a bowl.
2. Soak the chicken in the sauce for 30 minutes.
3. Cover the skillet.
4. Set to manual.
5. Cook at high pressure for 10 minutes.
6. Release the pressure quickly.
7. Choose the sauté button to thicken the sauce.

Nutrition:

Calories: 517
Fat: 26g
Protein: 10g

51. GARLIC AND LEMON CHICKEN DISH

Preparation Time: 11 minutes

Cooking Time: 18 minutes

Servings: 4

Ingredients

- 2-3 lb. chicken breast
- 1 tsp. salt
- 1 onion, diced
- 1 tbsp. ghee
- 5 garlic cloves, minced
- ½ cup organic chicken broth
- 1 tsp. dried parsley
- 1 large lemon, juiced
- 3-4 tsp. arrowroot flour

Directions

1. Set your skillet to sauté mode. Add diced onion and cooking fat.
2. Allow the onions to cook for 5-10 minutes.
3. Add the rest of the ingredients except arrowroot flour.
4. Lock the lid and set the skillet to poultry mode. Cook until the timer runs out.
5. Allow the pressure to release naturally
6. Once done, remove ¼ cup of the sauce from the skillet and add arrowroot to make a slurry.
7. Add the slurry to the skillet to make the gravy thick. Keep stirring well. Serve!

Nutrition:

Calories: 511
Fat: 29g

Protein: 11g

52. HIGH-QUALITY BELIZEAN CHICKEN STEW

Preparation Time: 7 minutes (+overnight prep)

Cooking Time: 22-23 minutes

Servings: 4

Ingredients

- 4 whole chicken
- 1 tbsp. coconut oil
- 2 tbsp. achiote seasoning
- 2 tbsp. white vinegar
- 3 tbsp. Worcestershire sauce
- 1 cup yellow onion, sliced
- 3 garlic cloves, sliced
- 1 tsp. ground cumin
- 1 tsp. dried oregano
- ½ tsp. black pepper
- 2 cups chicken stock

Directions

1. Take a large-sized bowl and add achiote paste, vinegar, Worcestershire sauce, oregano, cumin, and pepper. Mix well and add chicken pieces and rub the marinade all over them.
2. Allow the chicken to sit overnight. Set your skillet to sauté mode and add coconut oil.
3. Once hot, cook chicken pieces on the skillet in batches. Remove the seared chicken and transfer them to a plate.
4. Add onions, garlic to the skillet and sauté for 2-3 minutes. Add chicken pieces back to the skillet.
5. Pour chicken broth into the bowl with marinade and stir well. Add the mixture to the skillet.
6. Seal up the lid and cook for about 20 minutes at high pressure.

7. Once done, release the pressure naturally. Season with a bit of salt and serve!

Nutrition:

Calories: 517
Fat: 21g
Protein: 9g

53. CRISPY MEDITERRANEAN CHICKEN THIGHS

Preparation Time: 9 minutes

Cooking Time: 30-35 minutes

Servings: 6

Ingredients:

- 2 tbsp. extra virgin olive oil
- 2 tsp. dried rosemary
- 1½ tsp. ground cumin
- 1½ tsp. ground coriander
- ¾ tsp. dried oregano
- 1/8 tsp. salt
- 6 chicken thighs (about 3 pound)

Directions:

1. Preheat the oven to 450°F. Line a baking sheet with parchment paper.
2. Place the olive oil and spices into a large bowl and mix together, making a paste. Add the chicken and mix together until evenly coated. Place on the prepared baking sheet.
3. Bake for 30 to 35 minutes.

Nutrition:

Calories: 491
Fat: 22g
Protein: 10g protein

54. GREEK PENNE AND CHICKEN

Preparation Time: 11 minutes

Cooking Time: 9-11 minutes

Servings: 4

Ingredients:

- 16-oz. package of penne pasta
- 1 lb. chicken breast halves
- ½ cup of chopped red onion
- 1½ tbsp. butter
- 2 cloves of minced garlic
- 14-oz. can of artichoke hearts
- 1 chopped tomato
- 3 tbsp. chopped fresh parsley
- ½ cup crumbled feta cheese
- 2 tbsp. lemon juice
- 1 tsp. dried oregano
- ground black pepper
- salt

Directions:

1. In a large-sized skillet over medium-high heat, melt your butter.
2. Add your garlic and onion. Cook for approximately 2 minutes.
3. Add your chopped chicken and continue to cook until golden brown. Should take approximately 5 to 6 minutes. Stir occasionally.
4. Reduce your heat to a medium-low. Drain and chop your artichoke hearts. Add them to your skillet along with your chopped tomato, fresh parsley, feta cheese, dried oregano, lemon juice, and drained pasta. Cook for 2 to 3 minutes.
5. Season. Serve!

Nutrition:

Calories: 411
Fat: 20g
Protein: 8g

55. CHICKEN AND RICE SOUP

Preparation time: 10 minutes

Cooking time: 34 minutes

Servings: 4

Ingredients:

- 6 cups chicken stock
- 1½ cups chicken meat, cooked and shredded
- 1 bay leaf
- 1 yellow onion, chopped
- 2 tbsp. olive oil
- ⅓ cup white rice
- 1 egg, whisked
- Juice of ½ lemon
- 1 cup asparagus, trimmed and halved
- 1 cup carrots, chopped
- ½ cup dill, chopped
- Salt and black pepper to the taste

Directions:

1. Heat up a pot with the oil over medium heat, add the onions and sauté for 5 minutes.
2. Add the stock, dill, rice, and bay leaf, stir, bring to a boil over medium heat, and cook for 10 minutes.
3. Add the rest of the ingredients except the egg and lemon juice, stir and cook for 15 minutes more.
4. Add the egg whisked with the lemon juice gradually.
5. Whisk the soup, cook for 2 minutes more, divide into bowls, and serve.

Nutrition:

Calories: 263
Fat: 18.5g
Fiber: 4.5g
Carbs: 19.8g
Protein: 14.5g

CHAPTER NINE

SEAFOOD RECIPES

56. SAVORY CILANTRO SALMON

Preparation Time: 10 minutes

Cooking Time: 32-34 minutes

Servings: 4

Ingredients:

- 2 tbsp. of fresh lime or lemon
- 4 cups of fresh cilantro, divided
- 2 tbsp. hot red pepper sauce
- ½ tsp. salt, divided
- 1 tsp. of cumin
- 4 7-oz. salmon filets
- ½ cup (4 oz.) water
- 2 cups sliced red bell pepper
- 2 cups sliced yellow bell pepper
- 2 cups sliced green bell pepper
- Cooking spray
- ½ tsp. pepper

Directions:

1. Get a blender or food processor and combine half of the cilantro, lime juice or lemon, cumin, hot red pepper sauce, water, and salt. Puree until smooth. Transfer the marinade into a large, resealable plastic bag.
2. Add salmon to marinade. Seal the bag, squeeze out air that might have been trapped inside, turn to coat salmon.
3. After marinating, preheat your oven to about 400°F. Arrange the pepper slices in a single layer in a slightly-greased, medium-sized square baking dish. Bake it for 20 minutes, turn the pepper slices once.
4. Drain your salmon and do away with the marinade. Crust the upper part of the salmon with the remaining chopped, fresh cilantro.
5. Place salmon on the top of the pepper slices and bake for about 12-14 minutes until you observe the fish flakes easily when tested with a fork.

Nutrition:

Calories: 350
Fat: 13g
Protein: 42g

57. SALMON FLORENTINE

Preparation Time: 5 minutes

Cooking Time: 30 minutes

Servings: 4

Ingredients:

- 1½ cups chopped cherry tomatoes
- ½ cup chopped green onions
- 2 garlic cloves, minced
- 1 tsp. olive oil
- 1 quantity of 12 oz. package frozen chopped spinach, thawed and patted dry
- ¼ tsp. crushed red pepper flakes
- ½ cup part-skim ricotta cheese
- ¼ tsp. each for pepper and salt
- 4 5½-oz. wild salmon fillets
- Cooking spray

Directions:

1. Preheat the oven to 350°F.
2. Get a medium skillet to cook onions in oil until they start to soften, which should be in about 2 minutes. You can then add garlic inside the skillet and cook for an extra 1 minute.
3. Add the spinach, red pepper flakes, tomatoes, pepper, and salt. Cook for 2 minutes while stirring. Remove the pan from the heat and let it cool for about 10 minutes. Stir in the ricotta.
4. Put a quarter of the spinach mixture on top of each salmon fillet. Place the fillets on a lightly greased, rimmed baking sheet and bake for 15 minutes or until you are sure the salmon has been thoroughly cooked.

Nutrition:

Calories: 350
Fat: 13g
Protein: 42g

58. ASPARAGUS AND SMOKED SALMON SALAD

Preparation Time: 15 minutes

Cooking Time: 10 minutes

Servings: 8

Ingredients:

- 1 lb. fresh asparagus, shaped and cut into 1-inch pieces
- ½ cup pecans, smashed into pieces
- 2 heads red leaf lettuce, washed and split
- ½ cup frozen green peas, thawed
- ¼ lb. smoked salmon, cut into 1-inch chunks
- ¼ cup olive oil
- 2 tbsp. lemon juice
- 1 tsp. Dijon mustard
- ½ tsp. salt
- ¼ tsp. pepper

Directions:

1. Boil a pot of water. Stir in asparagus and cook for 5 minutes until tender. Let it drain; set aside.
2. In a skillet, cook the pecans over medium heat for 5 minutes, stirring constantly until lightly toasted.
3. Combine the asparagus, toasted pecans, salmon, peas, and red leaf lettuce and toss in a large bowl.
4. In another bowl, combine lemon juice, pepper, Dijon mustard, salt, and olive oil. You can coat the salad with the dressing or serve it on its side.

Nutrition:

Calories: 159
Fat: 12.9g

Protein: 6g

59. SHRIMP COBB SALAD

Preparation Time: 25 minutes

Cooking Time: 7 minutes

Servings: 2

Ingredients:

- 4 slices center-cut bacon
- 1 lb. large shrimp, peeled and deveined
- ½ tsp. ground paprika
- ¼ tsp. ground black pepper
- ¼ tsp. salt, divided
- 2½ tbsp. fresh lemon juice
- 1½ tbsp. extra virgin olive oil
- ½ tsp. whole-grain Dijon mustard
- 1 (10 oz.) package romaine lettuce hearts, chopped
- 2 cups cherry tomatoes, quartered
- 1 ripe avocado, cut into wedges
- 1 cup shredded carrots
- 3 boiled eggs, diced

Directions:

1. Cook the bacon for 4 minutes on each side in a large skillet over medium heat till crispy.
2. Take away from the skillet and place on paper towels; let cool for 5 minutes.
3. Break the bacon into bits. Throw out most of the bacon fat, leaving behind only 1 tbsp. in the skillet.
4. Bring the skillet back to medium-high heat. Add black pepper and paprika to the shrimp for seasoning. Cook the shrimp for around 2 minutes on each side until it is opaque. Sprinkle with ⅛ tbsp. of salt for seasoning.

5. Combine the remaining ⅛ tbsp. of salt, mustard, olive oil, and lemon juice together in a small bowl. Stir in the romaine hearts.
6. On each serving plate, place 1½ cups of romaine lettuce. Add on top the same amounts of avocado, carrots, boiled eggs, tomatoes, shrimp, and bacon.

Nutrition:

Calories: 528
Fat: 28.7g
Protein: 49g

60. TOAST WITH SMOKED SALMON, HERBED CREAM CHEESE, AND GREENS

Preparation Time: 10 minutes

Cooking Time: 5 minutes

Servings: 2

Ingredients:

For the herbed cream cheese:

- ¼ cup cream cheese, at room temperature
- 2 tbsp. chopped fresh flat-leaf parsley
- 2 tbsp. chopped fresh chives or sliced scallion
- ½ tsp. garlic powder
- ¼ tsp. kosher salt

For the toast:

- 2 slices bread
- 4 oz. smoked salmon
- A small handful of microgreens or sprouts
- 1 tbsp. capers, drained and rinsed
- ¼ small red onion, very thinly sliced

Directions:

To make the herbed cream cheese:

1. In a small container, put together the cream cheese, parsley, chives, garlic powder, and salt.
2. Using a fork, mix until combined.
3. Chill until ready to use.

To make the toast:

1. Toast the bread until golden.
2. Spread the herbed cream cheese over each piece of toast, then top with the smoked salmon.
3. Garnish with the microgreens, capers, and red onion.

Nutrition:

Calories: 194
Fat: 8g
Protein: 12g

61. MACKEREL AND GREEN BEAN SALAD

Preparation Time: 10 minutes

Cooking Time: 11 minutes

Serving: 2

Ingredients:

- 2 cups green beans
- 1 tbsp. avocado oil
- 2 mackerel fillets
- 4 cups mixed salad greens
- 2 hard-boiled eggs, sliced
- 1 avocado, sliced
- 2 tbsp. lemon juice
- 2 tbsp. olive oil
- 1 tsp. Dijon mustard
- Salt and black pepper, to taste

Directions:

1. Cook the green beans in a pot of boiling water for about 3 minutes. Drain and set aside.
2. Melt the avocado oil in a pan over medium heat. Add the mackerel fillets and cook each side for 4 minutes.
3. Divide the greens between two salad bowls. Top with the mackerel, sliced egg, and avocado slices.
4. Scourge lemon juice, olive oil, mustard, salt, and pepper, and drizzle over the salad. Add the cooked green beans and toss to combine, then serve.

Nutrition:

Calories: 737
Fat: 57g

Protein: 34g
Carbs: 45g

62. FISH AND ORZO

Preparation time: 10 minutes

Cooking time: 35 minutes

Servings: 4

Ingredients:

- 1 tsp. garlic, minced
- 1 tsp. red pepper, crushed
- Two shallots, chopped
- 1 tbsp. olive oil
- 1 tsp. anchovy paste
- 1 tbsp. oregano, chopped
- 2 tbsp. black olives, pitted and chopped
- 2 tbsp. capers, drained
- 15 oz. canned tomatoes, crushed
- A pinch of salt and black pepper
- Four cod fillets, boneless
- 1-oz. feta cheese, crumbled
- 1 tbsp. parsley, chopped
- 3 cups chicken stock
- 1 cup orzo pasta
- Zest of 1 lemon, grated

Directions:

1. Heat a pan and put the oil over medium heat; add the garlic, red pepper, and shallots and sauté for 5 minutes.
2. Add the anchovy paste, oregano, black olives, capers, tomatoes, salt, and pepper, stir and cook for 5 minutes more.
3. Add the cod fillets, sprinkle the cheese and parsley on top, place in the oven, and bake at 375°F for 15 minutes.

4. Put the stock in a pot, bring to a boil over medium heat, add the orzo and lemon zest, bring to a simmer, cook for 10 minutes, fluff with a fork, and divide between plates.
5. Top each serving with the fish mix and serve.

Nutrition:

Calories: 402
Fat: 21g
Protein: 31g
Fiber: 8g
Carbs: 21g

63. BAKED SEA BASS

Preparation time: 10 minutes

Cooking time: 12 minutes

Servings: 4

Ingredients:

- 4 sea bass fillets, boneless
- Salt and black pepper to the taste
- 2 cups potato chips, crushed
- 1 tbsp. mayonnaise

Directions:

1. Put seasonings on the fish fillets with salt and pepper, brush with the mayonnaise, and dredge each in the potato chips.
2. Arrange the fillets on a baking sheet lined with parchment paper and bake at 400°F for 12 minutes.
3. Divide the fish between plates and serve with a side salad.

Nutrition:

Calories: 228
Fat: 8.6g
Fiber: 0.6g
Carbs: 9.3g
Protein: 25g

64. FISH AND TOMATO SAUCE

Preparation time: 10 minutes

Cooking time: 30 minutes

Servings: 4

Ingredients:

- 4 cod fillets, boneless
- 2 garlic cloves, minced
- 2 cups cherry tomatoes, halved
- 1 cup chicken stock
- A pinch of salt and black pepper
- ¼ cup basil, chopped

Directions:

1. Put the tomatoes, garlic, salt, and pepper in a pan, heat up over medium heat, and cook for 5 minutes.
2. Add the fish and rest of the ingredients, bring to a simmer, cover the pan, and cook for 25 minutes.
3. Divide the mix between plates and serve.

Nutrition:

Calories: 180
Fat: 1.9g
Fiber: 1.4g
Carbs: 5.3g
Protein: 33.8g

65. OLIVE OIL POACHED COD

Preparation time: 5 minutes.

Cooking time: 6 minutes.

Servings: 4.

Ingredients:

- 2 tsp. of lemon juice
- 4-6 oz. of cod fillets
- 3 cups of olive oil
- 1 tsp. of lemon zest
- 1 tbsp. of salt

Directions:

1. Wash the fillets and put them on a paper towel.
2. Put oil inside a big pot, add the fish fillets to poach for about 6 minutes, or when the fish color changes to opaque.
3. Take the fish out of the oil and add salt to it. Put some of the leftover warm oil on the fish, add lemon juice to it. Add zest by sprinkling. It is ready to be served.

Nutrition:

Calories: 305
Fat: 15g
Protein: 31g
Carbs: 10g

66. PISTACHIO-CRUSTED HALIBUT

Preparation Time: 15 minutes

Cooking Time: 20 minutes

Servings: 4

Ingredients:

- 4-6 oz. halibut fillets with skin removed
- ½ cup shelled unsalted pistachios, chopped
- 4 tsp. fresh parsley, chopped
- 1 cup bread crumbs
- ¼ cup extra virgin olive oil
- 2 tsp. grated orange zest
- 1 tsp. grated lime zest
- ½ tsp. pepper
- 4 tsp. Dijon mustard
- 1½ tsp. salt

Directions:

1. Preheat the oven to 400°F.
2. In the food processor, add pistachio, zest, bread crumbs, parsley, and oil. Pulse until the ingredients are well-combined.
3. Rinse the fish and pat dry with a paper towel. Season the fillet with salt and pepper.
4. Brush the fish with mustard and divide the pistachio mix evenly with some on top of the fish. Press down the mixture to allow the crust to adhere.
5. Lining the baking sheet with crusted paper, arrange the crusted fish, and bake for 20 minutes or until the fillet is golden brown.
6. Leave for 5 minutes to cool, and then serve.

Nutrition:

Calories: 231
Fat: 9.5g
Carbs: 31.5g
Protein: 5.8g

67. CRAB MELT WITH AVOCADO AND EGG

Preparation Time: 15 minutes

Cooking Time: 15 minutes

Servings: 2

Ingredients:

- 2 English muffins, split
- 3 tbsp. butter, divided
- 2 tomatoes, cut into slices
- 1 (4-oz.) can lump crabmeat
- 6 oz. sliced or shredded cheddar cheese
- 4 large eggs
- Kosher salt
- 2 large avocados, halved, pitted, and cut into slices
- Microgreens, for garnish

Directions:

1. Preheat the broiler.
2. Toast the English muffin halves. Place the toasted halves, cut-side up, on a baking sheet.
3. Spread 1½ tsp. of butter evenly over each half, allowing the butter to melt into the crevices. Top each with tomato slices, then divide the crab over each and finish with the cheese.
4. Boil for about 4 minutes until the cheese melts.
5. Meanwhile, in a medium skillet over medium heat, melt the remaining 1 tbsp. of butter, swirling to coat the bottom of the skillet. Crack the eggs into the skillet, giving ample space for each. Sprinkle with salt. Cook for about 3 minutes. Turn the eggs and cook the other side until the yolks are set to your liking. Place an egg on each English muffin half.
6. Top with avocado slices and microgreens.

Nutrition:

Calories: 222
Fat: 84g
Protein: 12g

68. CRISPY POTATOES WITH SMOKED SALMON, KALE, AND HOLLANDAISE-STYLE SAUCE

Preparation Time: 15 minutes

Cooking Time: 15 minutes

Servings: 2

Ingredients:

- 2 tbsp. extra virgin olive oil, plus additional for preparing the baking sheet
- ½ recipe roasted potatoes
- 8 oz. mushrooms, stemmed and sliced
- 1 garlic clove, minced
- 8 oz. kale, thick stems removed, leaves cut into 2-inch pieces
- Kosher salt
- Freshly ground black pepper
- ½ recipe Hollandaise-Style Sauce, at room temperature
- 8 oz. smoked salmon

Directions:

1. Preheat the oven to 400°F. Lightly coat a baking sheet with oil.
2. Place the roasted potatoes on the prepared baking sheet and heat until warm.
3. Heat the oil over medium heat until it shimmers. Add the mushrooms and sauté for about 4 minutes until softened. Add the garlic and cook for 30 seconds. Add the kale and sauté for about 5 minutes until wilted and soft. Season with salt and pepper.
4. In a large bowl, combine the warmed potatoes, kale, and mushroom mixture. Toss to combine. Divide between 2 plates and spoon the sauce on top.
5. Nestle the salmon next to the vegetables on each plate and serve.

Nutrition:

Calories: 705
Fat: 42g
Protein: 15g

69. AVOCADO LIME SHRIMP SALAD

Preparation Time: 15 minutes

Cooking Time: 0 minutes

Servings: 2

Ingredients:

- 14 oz. of jumbo cooked shrimp, peeled and deveined; chopped
- 4½ oz. of avocado, diced
- 1½ cup of tomato, diced
- ¼ cup of chopped green onion
- ¼ cup of jalapeno with the seeds removed, diced fine
- 1 tsp. of olive oil
- 2 tbsp. of lime juice
- ⅛ tsp. of salt
- 1 tbsp. of chopped cilantro

Directions:

1. Get a small bowl and combine green onion, olive oil, lime juice, pepper, a pinch of salt. Wait for about 5 minutes for all of them to marinate and mellow the flavor of the onion.
2. Get a large bowl and combine chopped shrimp, tomato, avocado, jalapeno. Combine all the ingredients, add cilantro, and gently toss.
3. Add pepper and salt as desired.

Nutrition:

Calories: 314
Fat: 15g
Protein: 26g

70. SAVORY SALMON WITH CILANTRO

Preparation Time: 20 minutes

Cooking Time: 30 minutes

Servings: 4

Ingredients:

- 4 cups fresh cilantro (divided)
- 2 tbsp. fresh lemon or lime juice
- 2 tbsp. red pepper sauce
- 1 tsp. cumin
- ½ tsp. salt
- ½ cup of water
- 4 to 7 oz. raw salmon filets
- 6 cups bell pepper (all colors), seeded and julienned
- ½ tsp. pepper
- Cooking spray

Directions:

1. Place half the cilantro, lemon juice, red pepper sauce, cumin, salt, and water in a blender. Pulse the blender until smooth. Transfer into a Ziploc bag and place the salmon. Marinate inside the fridge.
2. Preheat the oven to 400°F. Arrange the bell peppers in a lightly greased baking dish. Sprinkle with pepper and bake for 10 minutes.
3. Drain the salmon and place on top the pepper slices and bake for 20 minutes.
4. Garnish with the remaining cilantro.

Nutrition:

Calories: 341
Fat: 0.1g

Protein: 1g

71. SHRIMP AND CAULIFLOWER GRITS

Preparation Time: 20 minutes

Cooking Time: 14-16 minutes

Servings: 4

Ingredients:

- 1 lb. raw shrimps, peeled and deveined
- ½ tbsp. Cajun seasoning
- Cooking spray
- 1 tbsp. lemon juice
- ¼ cup chicken broth
- 1 tbsp. butter
- 2½ cups cauliflower, grated or minced finely
- ½ cup unsweetened cashew milk
- ¼ tsp. salt
- 2 tbsp. sour cream
- ⅓ cup reduced-fat shredded cheddar cheese
- ¼ cup sliced scallions

Directions:

1. Place the shrimps and Cajun seasonings into a Ziploc bag and close the bag. Toss to coat the shrimps evenly with the seasoning.
2. Spray a skillet with cooking spray and cook the seasoned shrimps until pink. This will take about 2 to 3 minutes per side. Add the lemon juice and chicken broth. Make sure to scrape the bottom to remove the browned bits. Set aside.
3. In another skillet, heat butter over a medium flame and add the rice cauliflower. Cook for 5 minutes and add the milk and salt. Cook for another 5 minutes. Remove from the heat and add the sour cream and cheese. Stir until well-combined.
4. Serve the shrimps on top of the cauliflower grits.

5. Garnish with scallions.

Nutrition:

Calories: 456
Fat: 3g
Protein: 2g

72. TUNA NIÇOISE SALAD

Preparation Time: 20 minutes

Cooking Time: 25 minutes

Servings: 4

Ingredients:

- 4 tsp. extra virgin olive oil
- 3 tbsp. balsamic vinegar
- 2 garlic cloves (minced)
- 6 cups mixed greens
- 2 cups string beans (steamed)
- 1 cup cherry tomatoes (halved)
- 6 hard-boiled eggs (sliced)
- 2 7-oz. cans of tuna, packed in water and drained

Directions:

1. Mix the oil, vinegar, and garlic in a bowl until well-combined.
2. Place the remaining ingredients in a bowl and drizzle with the prepared sauce.

Nutrition:

Calories: 392
Fat: 1g
Protein: 2g

73. SHRIMP & ZUCCHINI

Preparation Time: 20 minutes

Cooking Time: 11-13 minutes

Servings: 4

Ingredients:

- 1 lb. shrimp, peeled and deveined
- 1 zucchini (chopped)
- 1 summer squash (chopped)
- 2 tbsp. olive oil
- ½ small onion (chopped)
- ½ tsp. paprika
- ½ tsp. garlic powder
- ½ tsp. onion powder
- Pepper
- Salt

Directions:

1. In a bowl, mix paprika, garlic powder, onion powder, pepper, and salt. Add shrimp and toss well.
2. Heat 1 tbsp. of oil in a pan over medium heat.
3. Add shrimp and cook for 2 minutes on each side or until shrimp turns pink.
4. Transfer shrimp on a plate.
5. Add remaining oil to a pan.
6. Add onion, summer squash, and zucchini, then cook for 6-8 minutes or until vegetables are softened.
7. Return shrimp to the pan and cook for 1 minute.
8. Serve and enjoy.

Nutrition:

Calories: 215
Fat: 0.5g
Protein: 1g

74. LEMON-ROSEMARY SALMON STEAKS

Preparation Time: 15 minutes

Cooking Time: 20 minutes

Servings: 2

Ingredients:

- 1 tbsp. lemon juice
- ½ tbsp. of dried rosemary
- 1 tbsp. of extra virgin olive oil
- 4 (6-oz.) wild salmon fillets from the Pacific
- Salt and black chili pepper, to taste

Directions:

1. Preheat to 350°F on the burner. Combine to a medium baking dish lemon juice, olive oil, and rosemary.
2. Season salmon fillets with salt and pepper. Add fillets to the baking dish, turn to coat, and allow to marinate for 10 to 15 min.
3. Cover foil dish and bake for about 20 minutes until the fish flakes easily with a fork. Take out of the oven and serve.

Nutrition:

Calories: 336
Fat: 9g
Protein: 6g

75. SHRIMP WITH DIPPING SAUCE

Preparation Time: 5 minutes

Cooking Time: 5 minutes

Servings: 6

Ingredients:

- 1 tbsp. reduced-sodium soy sauce
- 2 tsp. hot pepper sauce
- 1 tsp. olive oil
- ¼ tsp. garlic powder
- ⅛-¼ tsp. cayenne pepper
- 1 lb. uncooked medium shrimp, peeled and deveined
- 2 tbsp. chopped green onions

Dipping sauce:

- 3 tbsp. reduced-sodium soy sauce
- 1 tsp. rice vinegar
- 1 tbsp. orange juice
- 2 tsp. sesame oil
- 2 tsp. honey
- 1 garlic clove (minced)
- 1½ tsp. minced fresh ginger root

Directions:

1. Heat the initial 5 ingredients in a big nonstick frying pan for 30 seconds, then mix continuously.
2. Add onions and shrimp and stir fry for 4-5 minutes, or until the shrimp turns pink.
3. Mix the sauce and serve with the shrimp.

Nutrition:

Calories: 97
Fat: 4g
Protein: 2g

76. LEMON-GARLIC SHRIMP WITH ASPARAGUS

Preparation Time: 5 minutes

Cooking Time: 15 minutes

Servings: 6

Ingredients:

- Red bell peppers, chopped and planted
- 2 tbsp. of asparagus, cut into 1-inch bits
- 2 tsp. lemon zest
- ½ tsp. salt
- 2 tbsp. extra virgin olive oil
- 5 cloves of garlic, peeled and chopped
- 1 lb. of big, shelled, and deveined raw shrimp
- 1 cup chicken broth low in sodium
- 1 tbsp. cornstarch
- 1 tbsp. lemon juice
- 2 tbsp. of fresh chopped parsley

Directions:

1. Cover a big, non-stick skillet over medium-high heat with cooking spray and warm.
2. Add asparagus, bell peppers, lemon zest, and ¼ tsp. salt. Stir until vegetables start softening, around 6 minutes. Move vegetables, cover, and set aside in a tub.
3. Stir in the pan with oil and garlic and sauté for 30 seconds. Stir in some shrimps. Combine broth and cornstarch and whisk in a small bowl. Stir the broth mixture and the remaining ¼ tsp. salt into the saucepan.
4. Cook, stirring frequently for about 2 to 3 minutes, until sauce thickens and shrimps are pink and cooked through. Remove the

saucepan from heat, adding lemon juice and parsley. Play over the reserved vegetables and serve the shrimp.

Nutrition:

Calories: 351
Fat: 16g
Protein: 10g

77. CREAMY FETTUCCINE WITH SCALLOPS

Preparation Time: 5 minutes

Cooking Time: 9 minutes

Servings: 4

Ingredients

- Salt and black chili pepper, to taste
- 8-oz. whole-wheat fettuccine
- 1 lb. of big scallops at sea
- 1 (8-oz.) bottle of clam juice (lowest possible sodium)
- 1 cup of 2% milk
- 3 tbsp. of cornstarch
- 3 cups frozen peas
- ⅓ cup of chopped peppers
- ½ tsp. zest of lemon
- 1 lemon juice in a tsp.
- ½ cup Parmesan grated cheese

Directions:

1. Pick up a big pot of lightly salted water over high heat to a boil. Cook fettuccine as instructed on the box. Drain the pasta and set aside.
2. Add a paper towel to dry scallops and sprinkle with salt. Cover a big, non-stick skillet over medium-high heat with cooking spray and warm. Add scallops and cook for around 2 to 3 minutes per side until golden brown. Remove from the pan and set aside.
3. Stir in the pan with clam juice. Put milk, cornstarch, salt, and pepper in a medium saucepan; whisk until smooth.
4. Pour the mixture into the saucepan and whisk with the juice of the clams. Stir continuously until sauce thickens, around 1 to 2 minutes, until the mixture is simmering.

5. For the clam sauce, add reserved scallops and peas and bring to a simmer. Mix well with reserved fettuccine, chives, lemon zest, lemon juice, and most cheese; remove the pan with remaining cheese from the oven and top pasta.

Nutrition:

Calories: 231
Fat: 14g
Protein: 9g

CHAPTER TEN

FRUITS, SWEETS AND DESSERTS

78. BANANA SHAKE BOWLS

Preparation Time: 5 minutes

Cooking Time: 0 minutes

Servings: 4

Ingredients:

- 4 medium bananas, peeled
- 1 avocado, peeled, pitted and mashed
- ¾ cup almond milk
- ½ tsp. vanilla extract

Directions:

1. In a blender, combine the bananas with the avocado and other ingredients, pulse.
2. Divide into bowls and keep in the fridge until serving.

Nutrition:

Calories: 185
Fat: 4.3g
Carbs: 6g

Protein: 6.45g

79. COLD LEMON SQUARES

Preparation Time: 30 minutes

Cooking Time: 0 minutes

Servings: 4

Ingredients:

- 1 cup avocado oil a drizzle
- 2 bananas, peeled and chopped
- 1 tbsp. honey
- ¼ cup lemon juice
- A pinch of lemon zest, grated

Directions:

1. In your food processor, mix the bananas with the rest of the ingredients, pulse well.
2. Spread on the bottom of a pan greased with a drizzle of oil.
3. Place in the fridge for 30 minutes, slice into squares, and serve.

Nutrition:

Calories: 136
Fat: 11.2g
Carbs: 7g
Protein: 1.1g

80. BLACKBERRY AND APPLES COBBLER

Preparation Time: 10 minutes

Cooking Time: 30 minutes

Servings: 6

Ingredients:

- ¾ cup stevia
- 6 cups blackberries
- ¼ cup apples, cored and cubed
- ¼ tsp. baking powder
- 1 tbsp. lime juice
- ½ cup almond flour
- ½ cup water
- 3½ tbsp. avocado oil
- Cooking spray

Directions:

1. In a bowl, mix the berries with half the stevia and lemon juice, sprinkle some flour all over, whisk, and pour into a baking dish greased with cooking spray.
2. In another bowl, mix flour with the rest of the sugar, baking powder, water, and oil, and stir the whole thing with your hands.
3. Spread out the berries, place them in the oven at 375°F, and bake for 30 minutes.
4. Serve warm.

Nutrition:

Calories: 221
Fat: 6.3g
Carbs: 6g

Protein: 9g

81. BLACK TEA CAKE

Preparation Time: 10 minutes

Cooking Time: 35 minutes

Servings: 8

Ingredients:

- 6 tbsp. black tea powder
- 2 cups almond milk, warmed up
- 1 cup avocado oil
- 2 cups stevia
- 4 eggs
- 2 tsp. vanilla extract
- 3½ cups almond flour
- 1 tsp. baking soda
- 3 tsp. baking powder

Directions:

1. In a bowl, combine the almond milk with the oil, stevia, and rest of the ingredients and whisk well.
2. Pour the mixture into a cake pan lined with parchment paper, place it in the oven at 350°F, and bake for 35 minutes.
3. Leave the cake to cool down, slice, and serve.

Nutrition:

Calories: 200
Fat: 6.4g
Carbs: 6.5g
Protein: 5.4g

82. STRAWBERRY ICE CREAM

Preparation Time: 10 minutes

Cooking Time: 20 minutes

Servings: 4

Ingredients:

- ½ cup stevia
- 2 lb. strawberries, chopped
- 1 cup almond milk
- Zest of 1 lemon, grated
- ½ cup heavy cream
- 3 egg yolks, whisked

Directions:

1. Heat up a pan with the milk over medium-high heat.
2. Add the stevia and rest of the ingredients. Whisk well.
3. Simmer for 20 minutes.
4. Divide into cups and serve cold.

Nutrition:

Calories: 152
Fat: 4.4g
Carbs: 5.1g
Protein: 0.8g

83. CINNAMON CHICKPEAS COOKIES

Preparation Time: 10 minutes

Cooking Time: 20 minutes

Servings: 12

Ingredients:

- 1 cup canned chickpeas, drained, rinsed, and mashed
- 2 cups almond flour
- 1 tsp. cinnamon powder
- 1 tsp. baking powder
- 1 cup avocado oil
- ½ cup stevia
- 1 egg, whisked
- 2 tsp. almond extract
- 1 cup raisins
- 1 cup coconut, unsweetened and shredded

Directions:

1. In a bowl, combine the chickpeas with the flour, cinnamon, and other ingredients and whisk well until you obtain a dough.
2. Scoop 1 tbsp. of dough on a baking sheet lined with parchment paper and repeat for as many cookies as you wish. Place in the oven at 350°F and bake for 20 minutes.
3. Leave them to cool for a few minutes and serve.

Nutrition:

Calories: 200
Fat: 4.5g
Carbs: 9.5g
Protein: 2.4g

84. COCOA BROWNIES

Preparation Time: 10 minutes

Cooking Time: 20 minutes

Servings: 8

Ingredients:

- 30 oz. canned lentils, rinsed and drained
- 1 tbsp. honey
- 1 banana, peeled and chopped
- ½ tsp. baking soda
- 4 tbsp. almond butter
- 2 tbsp. cocoa powder
- Cooking spray

Directions:

1. In a food processor, combine the lentils with the honey and other ingredients except the cooking spray and pulse well.
2. Pour the mixture into a pan greased with cooking spray, spread evenly, place in the oven at 375°F, and bake for 20 minutes.
3. Cut the brownies and serve cold.

Nutrition:

Calories: 200
Fat: 4.5g
Carbs: 8.7g
Protein: 4. 3g

85. CARDAMOM ALMOND CREAM

Preparation Time: 30 minutes

Cooking Time: 0 minutes

Servings: 4

Ingredients:

- Juice of 1 lime
- ½ cup stevia
- 1½ cups water
- 3 cups almond milk
- ½ cup honey
- 2 tsp. cardamom, ground
- 1 tsp. rose water
- 1 tsp. vanilla extract

Directions:

1. In a blender, combine the almond milk with the cardamom and rest of the ingredients, pulse well.
2. Divide into cups and keep in the fridge for 30 minutes before serving.

Nutrition:

Calories: 283
Fat: 11.8g
Carbs: 4.7g
Protein: 7.1g

86. BANANA CINNAMON CUPCAKES

Preparation Time: 10 minutes

Cooking Time: 20 minutes

Servings: 4

Ingredients:

- 4 tbsp. avocado oil
- 4 eggs
- ½ cup orange juice
- 2 tsp. cinnamon powder
- 1 tsp. vanilla extract
- 2 bananas, peeled and chopped
- ¾ cup almond flour
- ½ tsp. baking powder
- Cooking spray

Directions:

1. In a bowl, combine the oil with the eggs, orange juice, and other ingredients except the cooking spray, whisk well.
2. Pour in a cupcake pan greased with the cooking spray,
3. Place in the oven at 350°F and bake for 20 minutes.
4. Cool the cupcakes and serve.

Nutrition:

Calories: 142
Fat: 5.8g
Carbs: 5.7g
Protein: 1.6g

87. RHUBARB AND APPLES CREAM

Preparation Time: 10 minutes

Cooking Time: 0 minutes

Servings: 6

Ingredients:

- 3 cups rhubarb, chopped
- 1 and ½ cups stevia
- 2 eggs, whisked
- ½ tsp. nutmeg, ground
- 1 tbsp. avocado oil
- ⅓ cup almond milk

Directions:

1. In a blender, combine the rhubarb with the stevia and rest of the ingredients, pulse well.
2. Divide into cups and serve cold.

Nutrition:

Calories: 200
Fat: 5.2g
Carbs: 7.6g
Protein: 2.5g

88. ALMOND RICE DESSERT

Preparation Time: 10 minutes

Cooking Time: 20 minutes

Servings: 4

Ingredients:

- 1 cup white rice
- 2 cups almond milk
- 1 cup almonds, chopped
- ½ cup stevia
- 1 tbsp. cinnamon powder
- ½ cup pomegranate seeds

Directions:

1. In a pot, mix the rice with the milk and stevia, bring to a simmer, and cook for 20 minutes, stirring often.
2. Add the rest of the ingredients, stir, divide into bowls, and serve.

Nutrition:

Calories: 234
Fat: 9.5g
Carbs: 12.4g
Protein: 6.5g

89. BLUEBERRY STEW

Preparation Time: 10 minutes

Cooking Time: 10 minutes

Servings: 4

Ingredients:

- 2 cups blueberries
- 3 tbsp. stevia
- 1½ cups pure apple juice
- 1 tsp. vanilla extract

Directions:

1. In a pan, combine the blueberries with stevia and the other ingredients, bring to a simmer, and cook over medium-low heat for 10 minutes.
2. Divide into cups and serve cold.

Nutrition:

Calories: 192
Fat: 5.4g
Carbs: 9.4g
Protein: 4.5g

90. MANDARIN CREAM

Preparation Time: 20 minutes

Cooking Time: 0 minutes

Servings: 8

Ingredients:

- 2 mandarins, peeled and cut into segments
- Juice of 2 mandarins
- 2 tbsp. stevia
- 4 eggs, whisked
- ¾ cup stevia
- ¾ cup almonds, ground

Directions:

1. In a blender, combine the mandarins with the mandarin's juice and other ingredients, whisk well.
2. Divide into cups and keep in the fridge for 20 minutes before serving.

Nutrition:

Calories: 106
Fat: 3.4g
Carbs: 2.4g
Protein: 4g

91. CREAMY MINT STRAWBERRY MIX

Preparation Time: 10 minutes

Cooking Time: 30 minutes

Servings: 6

Ingredients:

- Cooking spray
- ¼ cup stevia
- 1 and ½ cup almond flour
- 1 tsp. baking powder
- 1 cup almond milk
- 1 egg, whisked
- 2 cups strawberries, sliced
- 1 tbsp. mint, chopped
- 1 tsp. lime zest, grated
- ½ cup whipping cream

Directions:

1. In a bowl, combine the almond with the strawberries, mint, and other ingredients except the cooking spray and whisk well.
2. Grease 6 ramekins with the cooking spray, pour the strawberry mix inside, place in the oven, and bake at 350°F for 30 minutes.
3. Cool and serve.

Nutrition:

Calories: 200
Fat: 6.3g
Carbs: 6.5g
Protein: 8g

92. VANILLA CAKE

Preparation Time: 10 minutes

Cooking Time: 25 minutes

Servings: 10

Ingredients:

- 3 cups almond flour
- 3 tsp. baking powder
- 1 cup olive oil
- 1 and ½ cup almond milk
- 1⅔ cup stevia
- 2 cups water
- 1 tbsp. lime juice
- 2 tsp. vanilla extract
- Cooking spray

Directions:

1. In a bowl, mix the almond flour with the baking powder, oil, and rest of the ingredients except the cooking spray and whisk well.
2. Pour the mix into a cake pan greased with the cooking spray, place it in the oven, and bake at 370°F for 25 minutes.
3. Leave the cake to cool down, cut, and serve!

Nutrition:

Calories: 200
Fat: 7.6g
Carbs: 5.5g
Protein: 4.5g

93. WATERMELON CREAM

Preparation Time: 15 minutes

Cooking Time: 0 minutes

Servings: 2

Ingredients:

- 1-lb. watermelon, peeled and chopped
- 1 tsp. vanilla extract
- 1 cup heavy cream
- 1 tsp. lime juice
- 2 tbsp. stevia

Directions:

1. In a blender, combine the watermelon with the cream and rest of the ingredients, pulse well.
2. Divide into cups and keep in the fridge for 15 minutes before serving.

Nutrition:

Calories: 122
Fat: 5.7
Carbs: 5.3
Protein: 0.4

94. PUMPKIN CREAM

Preparation Time: 5 minutes

Cooking Time: 5 minutes

Servings: 2

Ingredients:

- 2 cups canned pumpkin flesh
- 2 tbsp. stevia
- 1 tsp. vanilla extract
- 2 tbsp. water
- A pinch of pumpkin spice

Directions:

1. In a pan, combine the pumpkin flesh with the other ingredients, simmer for 5 minutes.
2. Divide into cups and serve cold.

Nutrition:

Calories: 192
Fat: 3.4g
Carbs: 7.6g
Protein: 3.5g

95. CHIA AND BERRIES SMOOTHIE BOWL

Preparation Time: 5 minutes

Cooking Time: 0 minutes

Servings: 2

Ingredients:

- 1½ cup almond milk
- 1 cup blackberries
- ¼ cup strawberries, chopped
- 1½ tbsp. chia seeds
- 1 tsp. cinnamon powder

Directions:

1. In a blender, combine the blackberries with the strawberries and rest of the ingredients, pulse well.
2. Divide into small bowls and serve cold.

Nutrition:

Calories: 182
Fat: 3.4g
Carbs: 8.4g
Protein: 3g

96. MINTY COCONUT CREAM

Preparation Time: 4 minutes

Cooking Time: 0 minutes

Servings: 2

Ingredients:

- 1 banana, peeled
- 2 cups coconut flesh, shredded
- 3 tbsp. mint, chopped
- 1 and ½ cups coconut water
- 2 tbsp. stevia
- ½ avocado, pitted and peeled

Directions:

1. In a blender, combine the coconut with the banana and rest of the ingredients, pulse well.
2. Divide into cups and serve cold.

Nutrition:

Calories: 193
Fat: 5.4g
Carbs: 7.6g
Protein: 3g

97. GRAPES STEW

Preparation Time: 10 minutes

Cooking Time: 10 minutes

Servings: 4

Ingredients:

- ⅔ cup stevia
- 1 tbsp. olive oil
- ⅓ cup coconut water
- 1 tsp. vanilla extract
- 1 tsp. lemon zest, grated
- 2 cup red grapes, halved

Directions:

1. Heat up a pan with the water over medium heat.
2. Add the oil, stevia, and rest of the ingredients, toss and simmer for 10 minutes.
3. Divide into cups and serve.

Nutrition:

Calories: 122
Fat: 3.7
Carbs: 2.3
Protein: 0.4

98. APPLE COUSCOUS PUDDING

Preparation Time: 10 minutes

Cooking Time: 25 minutes

Servings: 4

Ingredients:

- ½ cup couscous
- 1½ cups milk
- ¼ cup apple, cored and chopped
- 3 tbsp. stevia
- ½ tsp. rose water
- 1 tbsp. orange zest, grated

Directions:

1. Heat up a pan with the milk over medium heat, add the couscous and rest of the ingredients, whisk, simmer for 25 minutes.
2. Divide into bowls and serve.

Nutrition:

Calories: 150
Fat: 4.5g
Carbs: 7.5g
Protein: 4g

99. PAPAYA CREAM

Preparation Time: 10 minutes

Cooking Time: 0 minutes

Servings: 2

Ingredients:

- 1 cup papaya, peeled and chopped
- 1 cup heavy cream
- 1 tbsp. stevia
- ½ tsp. vanilla extract

Directions:

1. In a blender, combine the cream with the papaya and other ingredients, pulse well
2. Divide into cups and serve cold.

Nutrition:

Calories: 182
Fiber: 2.3g
Carbs: 3.5g
Protein: 2g

100. ALMONDS AND OATS PUDDING

Preparation Time: 10 minutes

Cooking Time: 15 minutes

Servings: 4

Ingredients:

- 1 tbsp. lemon juice
- Zest of 1 lime
- 1½ cups almond milk
- 1 tsp. almond extract
- ½ cup oats
- 2 tbsp. stevia
- ½ cup silver almonds, chopped

Directions:

1. In a pan, combine the almond milk with the lime zest and other ingredients, whisk, bring to a simmer, and cook over medium heat for 15 minutes.
2. Divide the mix into bowls and serve cold.

Nutrition:

Calories: 174
Fat: 12.1g
Carbs: 3.9g
Protein: 4.8g

101. STRAWBERRY SORBET

Preparation Time: 15 minutes

Cooking Time: 20 minutes

Servings: 6

Ingredients:

- 1 cup strawberries, chopped
- 1 tbsp. of liquid honey
- 2 tbsp. water
- 1 tbsp. lemon juice

Directions:

1. Preheat the water and honey until you get homogenous liquid.
2. Blend the strawberries until smooth and combine them with honey and lemon juice.
3. Transfer the strawberry mixture in the ice cream maker and churn it for 20 minutes or until the sorbet is thick.
4. Scoop the cooked sorbet in the ice cream cups.

Nutrition:

Calories: 30
Fat: 0.4g
Carbs: 14.9g
Protein: 0.9g

FINAL WORDS

With the Mediterranean diet, you will come closer to nature, as the entire food concept is dependent on fresh produce. Mealtime, in these lands, is nothing short of a celebration. People living in these parts have a tradition of eating together. It is time to nurture interpersonal relations as well.

It is the right time to start doing something that will not only improve your current state but will also give you a healthy future. After all, there is no more significant wealth than the health of an individual.

The primary aim of the Mediterranean diet is to make a person fit from within. Eating these foods will not only help enhance your outer physical appearance, but it will bring out a healthier inner glow. People with cardiovascular issues, blood pressure, blood sugar, stress, anxiety, and stomach-related ailments will benefit from this dietary program. Additionally, it will improve the development of brain cells and activity.

Keeping all these things in mind, it is safe to conclude that the Mediterranean diet will improve a person's immune system. Someone with a robust immune system will be able to resist diseases easily. Thus, your desire to lead a healthy, fulfilling and constructive life will be achieved successfully.

The goal was to provide a thorough look at this diet and all the advantages and disadvantages it can bring to your life. As always, when making dietary changes, you should consult your physician first to ensure this is a healthy change for you to achieve your health goals. Much research has supported the claim that the Mediterranean diet is the most efficient method to lose weight and improve one's overall health.

It is time to get rid of the bad and depressive feelings of the city and enjoy the colors and tastes that the true essence of the Mediterranean region can offer. We all know that Med is a region dedicated to the culinary arts, and it can seemingly bring out the hidden chef in us.

This book is dedicated to those who wish to learn more about Mediterranean ingredients—that includes the variety of colors, smell, and taste of the earth and sense of freedom and motivation that the region brings to life.

You have learned to appreciate and prepare delicious recipes based on the Mediterranean standard of food. You learned how to devise a variety of dishes that are authentically Mediterranean, which is humble and comforting but also imaginative.

Here, you learned how to use typical Mediterranean ingredients that are both easy to find and inexpensive. The recipes are simple, requiring very little time to prepare, so they are perfect for busy people. They all taste amazing and are sure to delight you and your family. However, should you feel extra creative, you can take on all of them and prepare them in various new and spectacular forms.

The Mediterranean diet is balanced with plenty of fruit and vegetables of many colors. This book was created to give all Mediterranean lovers a visit to the jewel of the kitchen. Many Mediterranean recipes, when properly interpreted, are a way to give you more energy and put you at ease. With this book, you will be able to enjoy delicious and healthy Mediterranean food in no time at all.

These recipes have been tried and tested by our friends and family to ensure that you get a product with only the most delicious and natural ingredients, nothing else.

The recipes you will find in this book are truly delicious, easy to prepare, and represent certified traditional Mediterranean cuisine, where all its flavors come from natural ingredients and are delivered by practitioners.

You will easily find within your fingertips the strength to settle and make this book your own. You have time to start preparing with this book already. The Mediterranean diet keeps us healthy and young. With the help of this book, you may help your family and the world to find a longer life and be more vibrant than before.

With this book, we wanted to provide a detailed look at the Mediterranean lifestyle and exactly what that entails. The more informed you are about this diet and exactly what you should and should not be eating, the greater your chances of success will be!

People love incorporating a Mediterranean lifestyle because of how user-friendly it is! There is no counting calories, decreasing your portion sizes, or counting your intake of macronutrients diligently all day. It's about learning what the diet entails and making the choice to fill your pantry and fridge with fresh, healthy ingredients to promote better health. You will be cutting out unhealthy things like processed foods, artificial sugars, refined grains, and soda from your diet, which are known to cause blood sugar spikes and excess weight gain. Instead, you'll be shopping for ingredients rich in vitamins, minerals, good fats, and antioxidants that will improve your health! With a menu allowing for whole grains, fish, seafood, fruit, vegetables, and even a glass of wine a day, the Mediterranean diet allows for a variety that you will not get sick of!

As long as you do this and stick to the simple rules of a Mediterranean diet, you can attain all the benefits it offers. One of the major benefits of this diet is that it is perfectly sustainable in the long run.

COLOR RECIPE IMAGES

We understand, you want recipes in this book with their color images. However, **if we add images of all recipes, the printing cost of this book will be too high** and it won't be affordable to all.

We wanted this book to be priced in a way that everyone can buy it. So, we decided not to add any recipe image in this book.

But this doesn't mean you can't access these images. To make it easier, **we've made IMAGES OF ALL RECIPES available in a PDF format which you can download anytime for free.**

The PDF has color images of all the recipes we listed in this book. **You can download the PDF by visiting to the below URL.**

www.nourishandclassychef.com/m-diet-images

Hope it helps.